Beyond Our World

How curiosity, creativity and courage
open new realms of possibility.

Rex Martyn

First published 2021 by Rox Martyn

Copyright text and illustrations © Rox Martyn, 2021

The moral right of Rox Martyn to be identified as the creator of this work has been asserted.

www.roxmartyn.com
hello@roxmartyn.com
@roxmartyn

Cover design by Rox Martyn
Internal design and typeset by Post Pre-press Group, Brisbane

ISBN 978-0-6452706-1-7 (hardcover)
ISBN 978-0-6452706-0-0 (paperback)
ISBN 978-0-6452706-2-4 (epub)

Well, hello there!

Thank you for being here,
on this page.

I have,
something to share,
in the hope it might be helpful for you.
Creativity changed my life.
This is the story of how,
I began again.

Rock Bottom,
in the darkness of depression,
revealed a window of opportunity,
to think, write and draw,
my way back up.

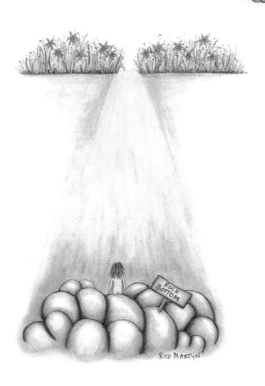

My eyes,
slowly adjusted,
to the chilling darkness,
of Rock Bottom.
I began to feel,
the atmosphere changing,
as buried thoughts stirred and surfaced.
I grabbed a pen and notebook,
to carry my words,
from heart, to head and hand.
A little oxygen breathing life into them.
Until I was swimming,
in an open sea,
of words.

The words,
began to make sense.
Doodles joined the party,
and they playfully danced,
into the still of night,
restless for a glimmering chance,
to explore the world,
beyond.

And so,
I gathered them up,
and popped them into this book,
to save myself, and them too,
from getting lost at sea,
in a storm of emotional grief,
and give them,
a new life.

My intent,
to begin with,
was to write a little 'life lessons' book,
for my newly born daughter,
Billie Grace.

Writing,
became enlightening,
uncovering something much bigger.
A buried treasure chest,
of golden nuggets,
and a lost soul,
Creativity.

Digging,
is how we uncover,
buried truths.
Chipping away persistently,
and patiently,
enabling,
hidden treasures,
to surface.

Windows,
of opportunity,
often float by softly,
riding a fleeting moment.
Notice when the air stirs around you,
jump on board with curiosity,
and see where it's going,
to take you,
today.

A hole,
I willingly descended,
was upon a rabbit.
Rabbit holes,
are wonderful places,
for chasing our restless curiosity,
around dark and winding tunnels,
searching for buried,
treasures.

Books,
make wonderful friends.
Written by our heroes of change,
they help us make sense of the world,
the subjects that matter to us,
and also make sense,
of ourselves.

Gratitudes,
to my book-friends,
their authors and illustrators,
for helping me to understand,
the enchanting realms,
and complex world,
of creativity.

Ruminating,
on the subject of creativity,
became therapeutic and enlightening,
helping to make sense of myself,
the rumbling discontent of lost truths,
and my long-distance relationship,
with creativity.

A wild imagination,
must never be caged.
Give it freedom to survive.
Let it soar the skies above,
and dive deep below,
hunting for nuggets of inspiration,
chasing sparks of curiosity,
to connect and engage with the world,
riding upon the seeds of ideas,
into unknown realms,
of possibility.

Beyond,
our familiar world,
is where our imagination explores,
the edges of possibility,
making the impossible possible,
and sprinkling a little,
creative magic,
everywhere.

An invitation,
awaits you right here,
to travel into the unknown.
Take hold and curiously unfold,
this map around the creative process.
Grab your wild imagination,
by the ears, horns, whatever's available,
and explore an inspiring world,
of creative discovery.

This book is for,

Creators.

Ordinary people like us,
making extraordinary things happen,
with curiosity, creativity,
and courage.

I do hope,
this beginning and evolving,
collection of considerations in creativity,
sparks something within you,
and speaks to you,
in some way.

And perhaps,
sprinkles a little creative magic,
into your world,
too.

Thank you,

This book is dedicated to my
beautiful daughter,

Billie Grace.

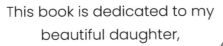

Thank you,
for sprinkling creative magic,
into my world.

Contents

Introduction

After twenty-five years of working in the creative fields of London, New York and Melbourne, I now teach and facilitate creativity in business and creative leadership. Based on first-hand experience and insights gathered from starting, managing and leading creative businesses, I wholeheartedly believe that creativity is our underdeveloped power for building a better future. The space at the intersection of creativity and business, between chaos and rigidity, within the contextual landscape of life, is where the creative magic happens. This is where I live and work; looking through this unique lens on the problems and challenges we encounter as individuals, teams and organisations.

If you're searching for answers, one way forward, a proven formula, or solutions on a silver platter, this isn't your book. If you're curious to explore a complex subject that will help you (re)discover your unique creative power and potential to transform life and become a (better) creator, then look no further. This is my attempt at making sense of the fuzzy ambiguity of creativity as a whole and turning the complexity and chaos into a useful concept – *a creative way of being* – that can be explored in many different ways.

This book is just the beginning. It's going to be incomplete because creativity is a complex subject; we are complex and unique individuals, navigating different, forever changing and complex circumstances, cultures and organisations, with common and distinctive problems and challenges. This is an attempt at unpacking the treasures of creativity and organising them into a useful framework to guide you around the creative process as an evolving collection of considerations. They seek to open your mind and expand your thinking to make space for more creativity to flow into your world and explore unfurling pathways to a whole world of possibility. There is no one way forward; there's a spectrum of options and you get to choose which way to go from here.

We have become very good at simplifying things for convenience. We turn our backs on inconvenient truths, put people in boxes, switch to autopilot, choose the quickest route and skim the surface, but it comes at a high cost to human creativity. Without embracing the ambiguity of a bigger picture – the enriching landscape of life – we struggle to gather inspiration, make interesting connections, cultivate novel ideas, become more fulfilled and make better progress. Whether we are under pressure to come up with 'the next big thing' or searching for something missing in our lives, when we unlock and develop our creative power and potential we open a whole world of possibility. Therefore, I prefer whole thinking, keyholes and opening doors to narrow thinking, stifling boxes and closed doors.

When creativity becomes the beating heart of our existence, as individuals, cultures and organisations, we will begin to make the change we seek. I think, therefore I draw. This is my way of making sense of life, creativity and business, and, through my unique lens, the things that matter and move us forward. Of course, the whole picture takes more time to explore, understanding the things that both help and hinder our creative progress; but only when these are on the radar can we confidently navigate the inevitable complexities and the meandering pathways to a better way forward. Therefore with one eye on the problem and one on the possibility, we make space for creativity to flow into our world and enrich our lives.

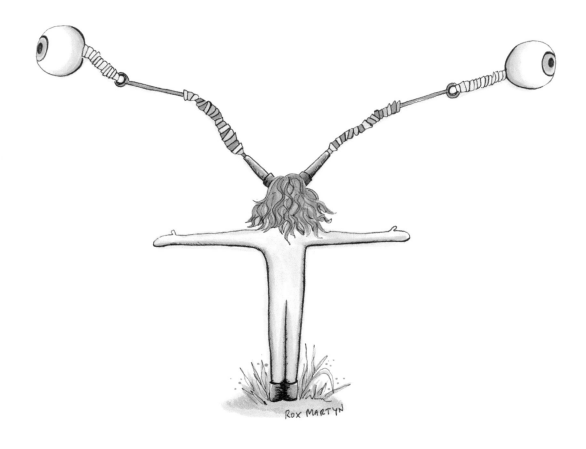

Five Realms

Creativity might feel out of reach for some. It's a fuzzy thing that's difficult to grasp. We might feel the rumbling discontent of neglected creativity within us, but struggle to entice it into the world beyond. Meanwhile, we might crave something more in life but can't put our finger on what that might be. Big ideas, hopes and dreams become a distant blur. An inspiration drought makes it difficult to come up with novel ideas, let alone make them happen. Old structures, systems and processes keep us on predictable pathways to nowhere different. This all paints a bleak picture for creativity.

I have found that creativity thrives within an encouraging contextual landscape. A place with freedom to explore, connect and engage, along with guidance, constraint and focus to work its wonderful magic. I created **Five Realms** to put creativity on the map for anyone seeking to become (better) creators and make creativity a better way of life. It's a creator's map: a sort of roadmap around the creative process as an engaging learning experience. It's an invitation to explore a world beyond our familiar landscape of everyday life, beyond the barren lands of our comfort zones and into new creative territory. The **Five Realms** is a place to explore and discover a whole world of creative opportunity.

The idea for **Five Realms** sprouted from an overflowing treasure chest of experiences and insights gathered from many years of working with creativity. A handful of golden truths highlighted a need for different thinking. I love maps and travel, so I blended this interest with the need for more creativity in our lives, and created a whimsical map for navigating the creative process. It's easy to grasp, navigate and adopt, and hopefully enjoy, no matter where you currently sit on the creativity scale.

The Golden Truths

Truth #1: Creativity is crushed by narrow thinking, old systems and processes.
The Realm Of Knowledge encourages us to expand our thinking with a contextual landscape that cultivates creativity.

Truth #2: Creativity is our underdeveloped human power.
The Realm Of Identity encourages us to embrace our individual creative power and potential.

Truth #3: Creativity withers without inspiration to spark our imagination.
The Realm Of Discovery encourages us to explore the bigger picture for interesting problems and challenges to fuel our creativity.

Truth #4: It's challenging to come up with bright ideas and then make them happen.

The Realm Of Creation encourages us to explore the edges of possibility to build meaningful creations.

Truth #5: Creativity struggles to deliver the goods without passion and power.

The Realm Of Progress encourages us to champion creativity to move our bright ideas and creations into the world.

Each realm is divided into three sections: painting a picture of our familiar world; the problems we encounter that prevent us from moving forward; and the possibilities for making change happen.

Your creative capacity

A good place to begin is right where you are. Here's a way to plot where you think you are today and highlight your scope for creative growth. Pop a dot on the scale of each realm, with 1 being the lowest score and 5 being the highest. Then join the dots together to make a shape. If you score 5 on all realms, you probably don't need this book. If you see room for creative growth, then you're off to a good start.

How to travel around the *Five Realms*

The intent is to begin in the middle, the barren lands of our comfort zone, and explore the **Five Realms** in order to complete the whole picture. That said, you can go in whichever direction grabs you. Just be aware that the areas you avoid are often the ones you need most. The realms are yours to explore and build upon, edit and tailor to what works for you. Travel them once, and then begin again to build upon your learning. This is just the beginning. It's your starting point to get those rusty cogs moving and creating wonders.

Constellation Of Competencies

A tiny minority,
rare breeds of lucky people,
are born naturally gifted geniuses,
on a ray of sunshine.

The rest of us,
breed of ordinary people,
have to learn and master new skills.
We put in the emotional labour,
grow our portfolio of skills,
to learn and patiently make,
extraordinary things,
happen.

Lucky for us,
creativity is a skill.
Which means it can be learned,
if we commit to the practice.
A constellation of skills,
perhaps better viewed as competencies,
will help us become,
better creators.

Creativity

*Because we need creativity integrated into
everyday life for human and cultural progress.*

We have unique creative power within us, but have underdeveloped
capacity and potential. Creativity helps us tackle the problems and
challenges of everyday life with bright ideas and meaningful creations.

Curiosity

*Because we need curiosity to discover new truths
and opportunities to nudge us forward.*

When we explore our interests, ask questions, dig deep, look
further and probe what we discover, we feed our creativity with
information, insights and inspiration that seeds novel ideas.

Connection

*Because we need to make connections that enable us
to grow and engage with the world.*

When we are connected to ourselves, the people around us, our culture and the
world we inhabit, we build a healthy ecosystem for cultivating our creativity.

Collaboration

Because we need collaboration to tackle challenges better together.

Effective, creative collaborations are a powerful force of change. Our individual power and potential, combined with our collective power and potential, enables us to tackle a complex spectrum of problems, and challenges, and explore diverse possibilities to create progress.

Courage

Because we need courage to wade through the unknown landscape of creative progress.

Without risk and uncertainty, vulnerability and courage, there is no human progress. Fear is paralysing to our progress, emotional exposure is tough. Yes we might fail, but we can dust ourselves off and try again because we will never know what we are capable of doing if we never try.

Critique

Because we need to critique the ideas we generate and build robust presentations.

We have remarkable imaginations, which means we have the potential to generate lots of novel ideas. At the same time we are bombarded with information, news, opinions and anything else that gets thrown our way. With this comes a greater need to analyse, interpret, evaluate and organise or we become overwhelmed in chaos.

Communication

*Because we need to communicate effectively to enable
us to connect and our voices be heard.*

As creativity has a tendency for fuzziness, chaos and confusion, it's vital that we learn to communicate our big ideas, perspectives and opinions in clear and concise ways. When communication breakdown happens, our ideas get lost in translation and entangled in messy landfill.

Compassion

*Because we need compassion to understand people,
to solve their problems and make life better.*

When we understand what life is like for others, identify their feelings and frustrations, we can extract the golden insights that feed our creative power and enable us to explore relevant solutions. And when working with others we must show compassion to encourage their creative efforts and contributions.

Commitment

Because we need commitment to learn, grow and progress.

We may have big dreams and good intentions, but without commitment we won't go very far. Creativity takes commitment to the practice, every single day, persistently and consistently, to become better, create better things, and go better places.

Contribution

Because the world is waiting for our creative contribution.

When we cultivate our creativity, every day, we become more confident and enthusiastic in sharing our ideas and creations. We all have unique creative power and when we make our contribution we add another dimension into the mix and expand our collective pool of possibility.

CHAPTER ONE

The Realm Of Knowledge

This chapter **paints a picture of a place** and a **creative process** that enriches your knowledge of the contextual landscape of creativity. It seeks to unlock and open your mind, expand your horizons and invite creativity into your world.

Navigate the **Realm Of Knowledge** and explore:

* The complex, diverse and distinctive nature of creativity.
* The contextual landscape in which creativity surfaces and grows.
* A creative process that inspires bright ideas and meaningful creations.
* Common barriers to creative learning and development.
* A bigger picture way of thinking and creating progress.

Because, when we know better, we become empowered to make better choices to grow in creative ways and go places in life.

Our Familiar World

World Of Creativity

In the past,
walls and doors,
were built to divide.
Today, we tear them down,
for social connection,
and integration.

Creativity,
isn't an exclusive club.
Everyone belongs in a world of creativity.
We all have keys, or the ability to make one,
and deserve the chance to step forward,
to open divisive, closed doors,
to connect and engage,
with the world.

Our Powerful Gift

Oh, creativity!
You can be mysterious,
magical and mighty.

Questioning,
whether we are, or not,
'creative people'.

But,
by default,
of being a human being,
like it or not,
we have creative treasures,
lurking somewhere within us,
along with an extensive imagination,
and the ability to unlock wonders,
our powerful human gift.
Creativity.

Our Creative Brain

Unfortunately,
it's *not yet* possible,
to nip to the local shop,
and buy an upgrade on our brain.
We have to work with what we have,
to enhance and develop,
its functionality.

By understanding,
that we engage our whole brain,
for creative thinking,
not just left or just right, but both sides,
we get to play a better game,
with creativity.

And so,
a bigger playing field,
enables novel connections,
to enter and enhance the game,
change the way we think,
and move.

Creativity Sandwich

Creativity lives,
in the space between,
imagination and invention.
Where the magic,
happens.

Think of it like,
a creativity sandwich.
Imagination. Creativity. Invention.
Together they make,
something,
bigger.

The sandwich,
breeds novel ideas,
of value to human evolution,
changing and shaping our lives,
expanding the landscape,
of human possibility,
and progress.

Bright Ideas

Bright ideas,
are born from little seeds,
embedded within the fabric and fibres of life.
What we now take for granted,
was once the twinkling,
of a big idea,
made possible,
by ordinary people like us,
doing extraordinary things,
with curiosity, creativity and courage,
to generously build ideas,
that shape a bright,
future.

Pressing Problems

Problems,
are scattered throughout the landscape,
of everyday life.
Obvious, hidden, small, big,
all shapes and sizes,
always calling for our attention,
waiting for someone with curiosity,
to notice and adopt them,
transform the problem into a solution,
a bright idea with good purpose,
bringing us hope,
and progress,
in life.

Making Space

Creativity,
needs space to surface,
to think, play, connect and grow.
A safe place where creativity belongs.
Where oxygen gives it life,
to explore its power and potential,
away from thick foggy chaos,
and nagging distractions.
Creativity thrives,
with space.

Embracing Ambiguity

Embrace,
our expanding world,
the transformative wonders,
and opportunities that await,
within our bigger picture.
Grasp ambiguity in life,
and find clarity,
within.

Creativity Is . . .

Walking,
into the unknown,
with curiosity, creativity and courage,
to cultivate bright ideas,
and lead the way,
forward.

Creativity Truths

The truth,
about creativity,
is that it's far from simple.
Like any meaningful relationship,
the key is connection.
But it's complex, and a constant,
work in progress.
Here are some truths,
to describe my relationship,
with creativity:

Complex
Mildly torturous (at times)
Unpredictable
Risk-taking
Paradoxical
Surprising
Nocturnal
Chaotic (if not organised)
Challenging
Adventurous
Brave
Determined
Playful
Engaging
Thoughtful
Generous
Humorous
Magical

How about you?

The Paradox Of Life

Life,
isn't a choice,
between one or the other.
A creative life,
embraces the paradox,
that creates a bigger landscape,
of possibility.

Powerful Intersections

Life,
and edges,
blend and blur.
It's not black and white,
or clear cut,
when we embrace the space,
and combinations unfolding,
in between.

Our interests,
talents, abilities and expertise,
can blend to become,
powerful creative intersections.
Leonardo da Vinci,
combined art and science,
to make an interesting lens on life,
opening a whole world,
of human possibility,
and progress.

Perfectly Imperfect

Imperfection,
is stepping forward,
with vulnerability and courage,
and being,
perfectly imperfect humans,
doing imperfect things,
within an imperfect world.
Living a creative life,
with what matters,
most.

Creative Equality

Creativity,
is a powerful human gift,
and right.
Creative equality,
matters.
As creative beings,
our truths and treasures rise,
upon waves of creative expression,
to connect, grow and engage,
with the world beyond.
Creative power,
to all people.

Engines Of Progress

Our power,
grows from connections,
becoming catalysts for change.
When three different fields of expertise,
like humanity, art and business,
become one integrated way of thinking,
working towards a greater good,
we create a powerful engine,
for human progress.

Wired For Connection

Human,
creative beings,
are wired for connection.
Our powerful creative hearts,
need to be carefully connected,
in a whole spectrum of ways,
sparking a flow of energy,
to engage with life,
and the world,
around.

The Problems We Encounter

Autopilot World

We inhabit,
an expansive and enchanting world,
of creative possibility.
But we're merely skimming the surface,
of our creative capacity,
and potential.

Life.
Busyness.
Productivity.
Switches us to autopilot,
defaulting to the quickest route possible.
Choosing certainty over uncertainty,
expected over unexpected,
same over different.
To land surely,
in the same,
spot.

Speed,
comes at a high cost.
We skip past our chance to discover,
novelty hiding in unexpected places.
We might venture off track,
perhaps get lost in the unknown,
but the golden treasures,
of a brighter outcome,
might just make,
a little deviation,
worthwhile.

Boxes, Boardrooms, Brainstorms

Stifle a human,
stereotype, label and stuff them,
into a convenient little box.
We have adopted,
this rather inhumane habit,
of putting people into suffocating boxes.
Because it's easier to control,
the conveniently stunned,
and stifled.

Individuality,
needs to surface.
Discover your true colours,
tap into that vibrant creative heart.
Say 'no' to labels and boxes,
places where creativity withers,
and bright ideas die,
under scrutinising stares,
within judgemental boardrooms,
deprived of daylight,
and oxygen.

BOARDROOMS & BOXES

ROX MARTYN

Corporate Entrenchment

Sometimes,
the way may already seem to be,
carved in heavy stone,
preventing us from going,
anywhere different.

But,
we do have a choice.
Conform and follow the crowd,
or escape the numbing entrenchment,
sniff the fresh air of realms beyond,
roam with curiosity around,
the meandering pathways,
where a better way,
awaits you.

Rox Martyn

The Merry-Go-Round

Creativity,
is easily sucked into distraction,
riding the merry-go-round,
to nowhere,
avoiding the fear,
that lurks in the unknown.
But creativity,
craves novelty, surprise and delight,
only found by exploring,
an enriching contextual landscape,
gathering golden nuggets of inspiration,
buried throughout new pathways,
to survive, connect, engage,
with the world.

Conformity Machines

One way,
to nudge us forward,
is to think about the alternatives.
We can choose to succumb and travel along,
the corporate conveyor belt of conformity,
more like robots than human beings,
moving along dazed on autopilot,
plopping out the other side,
calmly and conveniently,
into a little box.

Or,
we can escape,
the conveyor belt of convenience,
and choose to embrace life being human,
dance, explore, play and enjoy,
a life of curiosity, creativity,
and fulfilment.

Broken Systems

People,
and bright ideas,
fall through the cracks,
of archaic and broken systems,
restrictive and static structures,
processes and models.
Fix them, break them and rebuild,
something more useful.
Move with the times,
stay relevant and connected,
with structure and freedom,
to grow and make,
progress.

Layers Of Complexity

We live,
in a forever changing,
and complex world, with complex people,
with complex problems.
We could claim to have four worlds.
The world in our heads,
our familiar world around us,
the world beyond,
and the planet,
we inhabit.

And so,
our world of creative possibility,
is an expansive area,
from the edges of the bigger picture,
to the intricate, interwoven beauty,
of individual life,
within.

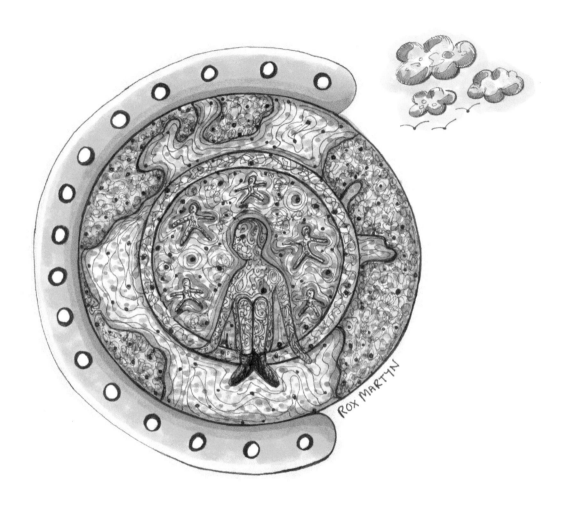

Oversimplification

Sometimes,
we oversimplify things,
just because, it's easier.
But it's likely to be,
unhelpful.

The art,
of simplicity,
lies in the balance between,
confusing, chaotic complexity,
and soulless oversimplification.
When mastering simplicity,
explore something,
less and more,
helpful.

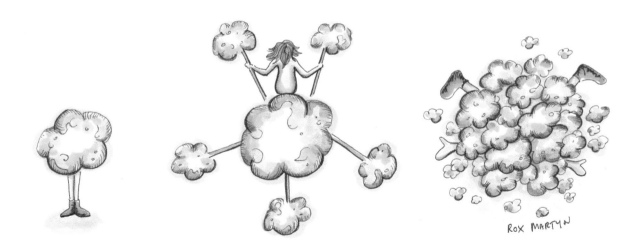

ROX MARTYN

Burnout

A state of being,
forever busy and on-the-go,
dashing around like nutters,
catching whatever gets thrown our way,
too busy to rest, reflect and refuel,
depletes the power and energy,
that fuels our creativity,
and is a fast way,
to burnout.

Disengaged

A sign,
of being disengaged,
is of no interest,
to you.

Elephants

It's heavy,
the atmosphere,
when the unspoken elephant,
plonks itself in the room,
stealing fresh oxygen,
blocking voices from rising,
stifling awkward conversations,
preventing the clearing of air,
the easing of tension,
that makes space,
for new thoughts and ideas,
to rise to the surface,
and play.

ELEPHANT IN THE ROOM ...   ROX MARTYN

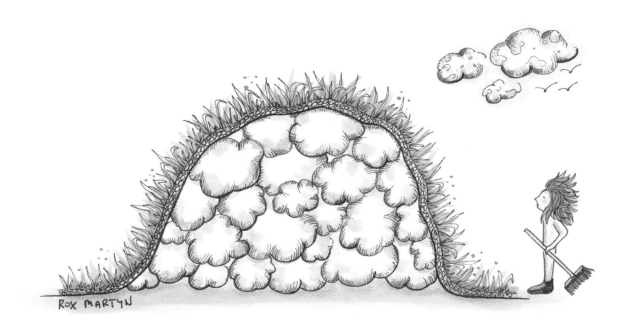

Under The Carpet

Thoughts,
unspoken words,
and festering feelings,
brushed swiftly under the carpet,
become a magnificent pile,
of inconvenient truths,
rising and blocking,
our way.

Playful Mistakes

Draw away!
This is your day.
Colour outside wobbly lines,
play with clumsy mistakes.
Because living in fear of doing,
brave and wild things,
will never show us,
the way forward.
Perfectionism,
doesn't belong here,
in the realms of progress,
and possibility.

Walking On Eggshells

Tip-toe,
here we go,
not too high or too low,
too fast or too slow.
Walking on eggshells,
living in fear of breaking,
big and delicate egos,
isn't how we learn,
leap forward,
and grow.

The Gap Of Discontent

And so,
here we are again,
teetering on the edge,
dreaming of going to better places,
beyond our predictable, familiar world.
But remaining stuck right where we are.
We can go much further in life,
if we choose the discomfort,
of human progress,
over gaping voids,
of discontent.

Getting Uncomfortable

Embarking,
upon exciting new adventures,
into the darkness of unknown realms,
is going to feel pretty weird,
and uncomfortable.
Without a doubt.

Because,
it's unfamiliar territory.
We have never been there before.
To land in new places,
and tread upon fresh ground,
we have absolutely no choice,
but to sit back, hold onto our chair,
and accept this is going to be,
uncomfortable.

Our Landscape Of Creativity

Unpacking Creativity

Creativity,
is a complex subject matter.
And so, it might be helpful to unpack,
its delightful treasures,
and organise them into five realms,
a guiding framework around the creative process,
an expansive and enriching experience,
where bright ideas surface,
and come to life,
with curiosity, creativity,
and courage.

Five Realms Of Creativity

Five realms,
of creative (re)discovery,
seek to open our minds,
challenge and expand our thinking,
to invite (more) creativity into our world.
Each realm is anchored by a principle,
and houses a collection of considerations,
to encourage creativity to rise to the surface,
become a way of being,
and making,
progress.

Anchor Principles

KNOWLEDGE
because when we know better,
we do better with a foundation of knowledge to build upon.

IDENTITY
because when we gain self-knowledge,
we connect with ourselves and grow in diverse ways.

DISCOVERY
because when we explore new landscapes,
we discover new opportunities to make a difference.

CREATION
because when we make bright ideas happen,
we make an impact with meaningful creations.

PROGRESS
because when we lead with curiosity, creativity and courage,
we influence change and progress.

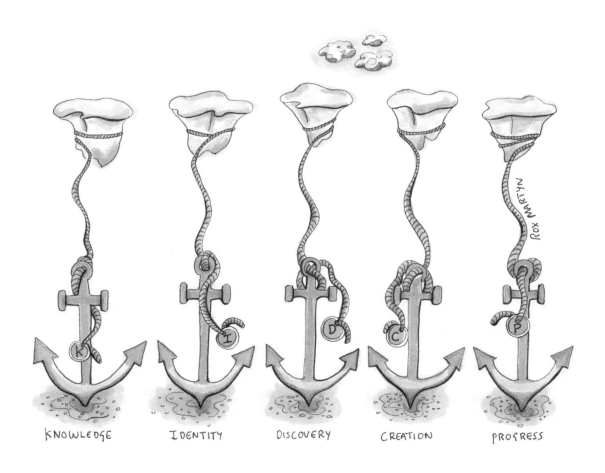

KNOWLEDGE   IDENTITY   DISCOVERY   CREATION   PROGRESS

A Creative Process

The word 'process',
seems to bring some folks out in a rash.
But creativity with good purpose,
is enriched and enlightened,
by the expansive pathways,
of a helpful process.

The problem,
is that not all processes are useful.
They can be restrictive and repetitive,
boring, frustrating,
uninspiring.

If the intent,
is to generate *novel* and valuable ideas,
within the context of our rapidly changing landscape,
then it might be a good idea,
to design a process,
that discovers,
novelty.

Enter,
five realms of creative discovery,
designed as an expansive and enriching experience,
creating space for novel connections,
to inspire *novel* ideas.
A whole contextual landscape,
that enables creativity,
to surface and work,
its magic.

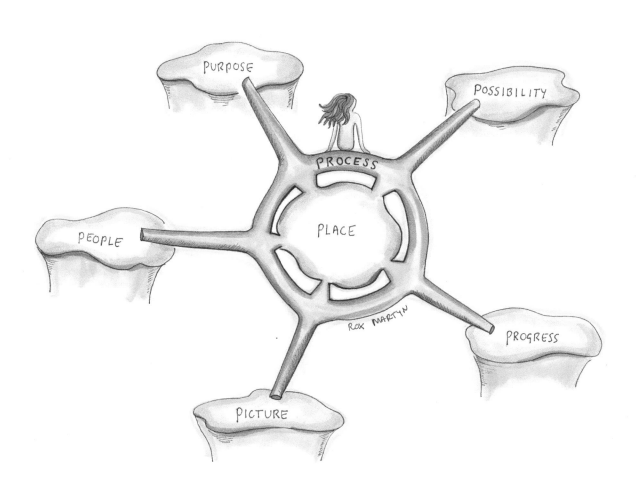

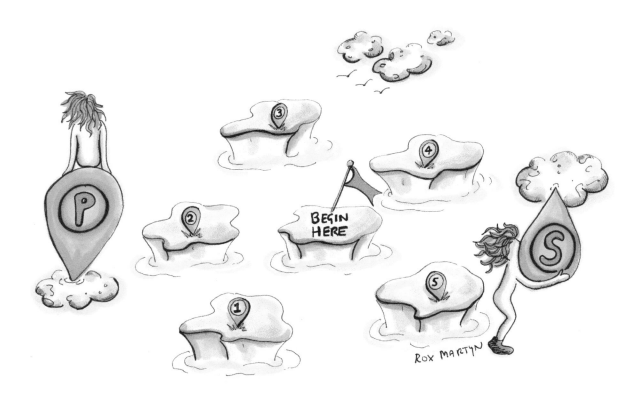

Problems To Solutions

Catch a problem,
and sprint with it to a quick solution.
Or travel together into new realms,
and land with an unexpected,
better solution.

Different Patterns

Different places,
emerge from different patterns.
By breaking the old,
and making something new,
we create pathways into the unknown.
It's easy to follow a repeat pattern,
keep doing what we've always done,
over and over, again,
remaining perpetually dissatisfied,
with where we land.
It takes far more effort and courage,
to break the norm,
explore somewhere different,
and commit to making,
a better pattern.

No One Way

There is no 'one way',
forward in life.
With all the complex layers,
people, places, problems, perspectives,
we encounter many ways.
The change we seek,
lights new pathways forward.
Our opportunity,
to engage our creative power,
expand and explore our potential,
uncovers fresh insights, inspiration and ideas,
nudging us into new territory,
to create a different,
perhaps better,
reality.

Creative Growth Mindsets

Open minds,
give us more space to explore,
and grow our brains in meaningful ways,
in many different directions,
to expand our thinking,
and explore our potential.
With diverse channels to transport,
our thoughts, feelings and findings,
our expansive brain radars,
tune into a bigger picture,
of possibility.

ROX MARTYN

The Map

Maps,
paint a picture,
of our contextual landscape,
to see what sparks our curiosity.
They show us where we are,
the places we want to go,
and different ways,
to get there.

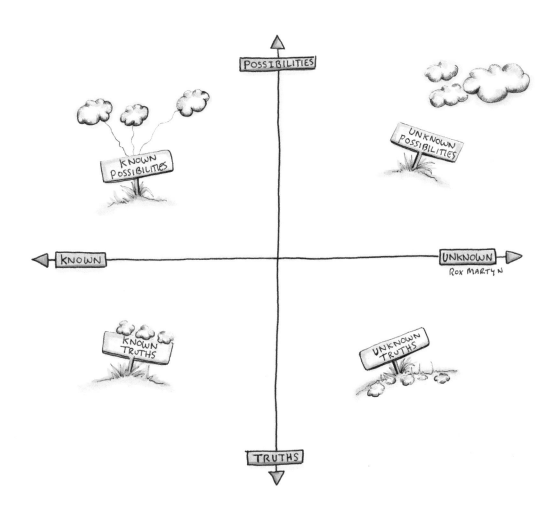

Changing Landscapes

Our landscape of life,
is rapidly and constantly changing.
Just when we think,
we've grasped something,
it's on the move,
yet again.

This is life.
Rather than retreat in fear,
of the inevitable shifting around us,
we can learn to keep better tabs,
on the moving parts.

By organising,
and observing them better,
we are positioned to notice and anticipate,
what's emerging, or calling for our attention,
and be open to jump onboard,
for the ride.

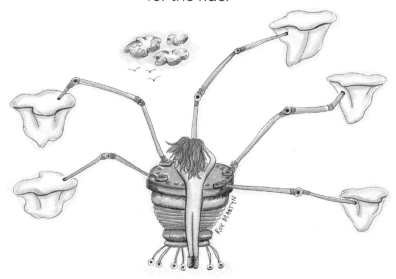

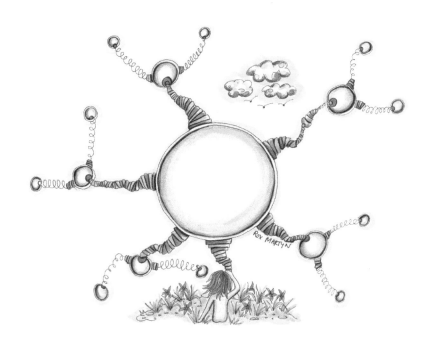

A Complex Lens

Oh world!
Forever evolving and expanding,
introducing new layers,
of complexity.

The thing is,
if we keep using the same old lens,
to observe a different and bigger picture,
we're not going to gain true perspective,
on the contextual landscape,
of our changing,
reality.

A complex world,
needs a better, more fancy,
(more sophisticated)
more complex,
lens.

Creative Ecosystems

For creativity,
to surface, survive and thrive,
we need to cultivate creative ecosystems,
that encourage connection and growth.
Where inspiration flows and ideas roam,
away from people, processes,
and places that stifle,
creative power.

Nature,
has inspired many bright ideas.
Ecosystems are one insightful place,
for learning and cultivating,
all things creative.

Kaleidoscope Of Possibility

With open eyes,
and through our creative lens,
we see a magical world of possibility.
Connections, patterns and combinations,
unfurling and frolicking before our eyes,
tiny bits that make an impressive whole,
challenge our existing world,
in search of new,
possibility.

Treasure Hunt

A game,
is a brilliant way,
to explore, discover and learn.
And let's face it, far more interesting,
than a boring old process.
So let the game begin!
Happy hunting for buried treasures,
and unexplored pathways,
that go places.

A World Of Possibility

Open,
new doors,
and step forward,
with curiosity, creativity and courage,
to explore and discover,
a whole new world,
of possibility.

Creativity Key

And so,
yes, everyone does,
have a mighty powerful key,
to a world of possibility,
with our unique gift,
of creativity.

Complete The Picture

Ignore,
the annoyingly persistent,
seductive power,
of convenience,
in disguise.

Autopilot,
has its place,
if we know our destination.
But if we want to go anywhere different,
and emerge with a different outcome,
something unexpected,
there is no place,
for autopilot.

Grasp,
a nifty map,
of creative discovery.
Identify,
the unexplored territory,
the missing pieces of the puzzle,
of the bigger picture.
Challenge,
our existing assumptions,
the way we think.
Enter,
into the five realms,
of creative discovery,
to complete you,
and your own,
picture.

Simple Tools

No magic tools here,
just a map, a roadmap if you prefer,
and a few simple, yet mighty, tools,
to keep us thinking on our feet.
Nothing fancy needed,
to get the job done.

NOTEBOOK
To jot down inspiration and doodle
random ideas as they appear.

JOURNAL
To record daily habits, practices,
experiences, thoughts and
encounters.

PENCIL/PEN
To scribble all thoughts from the heart,
head, hand and onto paper.

INSPIRATION POUCH
To collect golden nuggets of
inspiration as found.

MAP (five realms of creativity)
To keep on track with your adventures
of creative discovery.

CHAPTER TWO

The Realm Of Identity

This chapter focuses on **people, creative power** and **potential.** It seeks to unlock chambers of self-knowledge, digging beneath the surface to discover your hidden treasures and connect them with a whole world of possibility.

Navigate the **Realm Of Identity** and explore:

* Our wonderful individuality and unique creative power.
* Ways of expanding our creative capacity and potential.
* Ideas for growing with purpose and adopting creativity as a way of being.
* Common barriers to developing our creative power and potential.
* Ways of embracing your creative identity and exploring new possibilities.

Because, when we know ourselves better, we become connected to our power, a greater purpose and potential to engage with the world and become more creatively fulfilled.

Our Individual World

Human Individuality

Introspection,
is looking inwards,
with kindness and curiosity,
for hidden truths and treasures,
examining the intricate fingerprint,
of our human individuality,
noticing the weird little quirks,
and insightful patterns,
unfolding under the spotlight,
of our creative lens,
the vibrant magic infiltrating,
all human beings,
with distinctive and dynamic,
creative power.

Lifelong Beginners

Beginners,
are curious beings,
exploring and engaging with life,
trying new and brave things.
Knowing the unknown,
leads to different,
places.

Dip a toe,
into the chilly, murky waters,
easy does it.
Notice,
sensations slowly rising,
as thoughts and feelings stir,
and begin to surface,
a shiver of novelty,
the buzz of mixed emotion.
We belong,
where new beginnings await us.
Right here. Today. Now.
It's time to dip,
your toe.

From Within

Within,
glows with uniqueness.
What we hold deep inside,
close to our precious hearts,
seeps into everyday life,
creating energy,
inside out.
Embrace,
the dancing vibes,
feel them move and flow,
throughout your life,
into our world.

Creative Walnuts

Intelligence,
our creative walnut,
is a maze of pathways,
for creativity to explore,
and enrich our world.
Creative intelligence,
travels deep, far and wide,
making new connections,
weaving things together,
shaping who we are,
what we do in life,
and who we,
become.

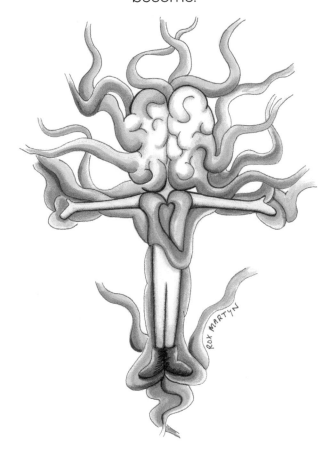

Emotional Intelligence

Intelligence,
without emotional connection,
is a lonesome brain,
without a heart.

Love,
is a life skill,
our brain and heart,
are waiting for us to learn,
the art of emotional connection,
explore the winding pathways.
Embrace a life of creativity,
meaningful relationships,
with compassion,
and courage.

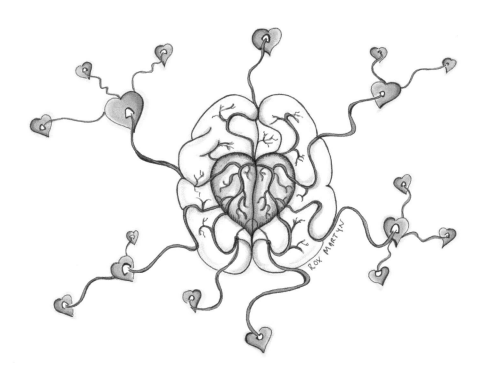

Human Needs

Needs,
we all have them.
Some are essential for survival,
like the need for food, shelter and clothes.
Other needs are for human fulfilment,
like adventure, connection, growth,
creativity and transcendence.
Our needs are more like,
interchangeable layers,
than static triangles,
always moving,
and evolving.

Digital Emotion

A while back,
emotions were hushed,
and brushed under the carpet.
Negative emotion was considered a weakness.
Today, thankfully, we know differently,
and get to play openly,
with an endless portfolio,
of entertaining, visual, digital human emotions.
There's an expression,
for every imaginable feeling,
unimaginable back then.
So go ahead,
browse away 'til your heart's content.
Take your pick and show us,
how you really feel,
and use emotion,
to connect,
and spark,
change.

Safety And Adventure

We embark,
upon brave creative endeavours,
with the security of safety and a sense of adventure.
Acknowledge fears and move on through them.
Navigate the risk, uncertainty and obstacles,
with vulnerability, courage and grace.
Brave the choppy seas of constant change.
Return triumphant with unexpected treasures.
This is how we make insightful discoveries for human progress,
with hidden truths, golden nuggets of inspiration,
sparking different thinking and novel ideas.
With safety and adventure,
we go further,
together.

Essential Hiding

Sometimes,
we have to hide away from life,
make space to nurture ourselves,
to fold into our creative heart,
for a little introspection,
and enrichment,
to grow.

Natural Growth

Here we grow,
within our natural ecosystem,
our evolving picture,
of human life.
Every year is precious,
telling a unique story,
of curiosity, creativity and courage.
So make each one,
count.

Creative Growth

Our brains,
powered by creativity,
grow in distinctive ways.
When we draw new patterns,
and flood them with colour,
we become creative stars,
of tomorrow.

Our Creative Heart

Creativity,
is the beating heart,
of a fulfilling human existence.
Pumping fresh blood and oxygen,
cultivating and carrying our bright ideas,
infiltrating our world with energy,
nourishing our juicy veins,
with creative magic.

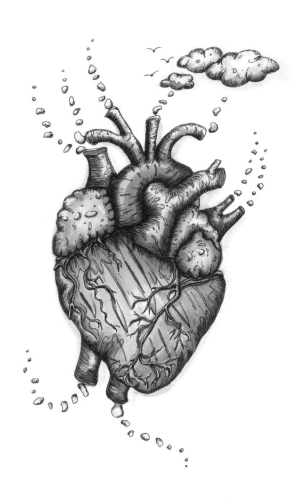

Wild Imagination

Wild imaginations,
are rocket fuel for creativity.
Transporting us into other worlds,
of impossible possibility.
Enabling,
the envisioning of things,
not familiar in the present.
Peek with curiosity,
through portals into alternative realms.
Imagine something different,
never seen before.
This extraordinary time capsule,
of the human mind,
travels backward and forward,
entertaining big dreams, wild ideas,
and unexpected encounters,
lurking around the unexplored edges,
of our imagination,
where novelty, surprise and delight,
feed our hungry creative power,
and cultivate bright ideas,
within our ecosystem,
of reality.

Our Perception

Our clever brains,
organise and interpret,
what we see.
Which might be different,
for you and me.
Take one famous example,
the 'duck–rabbit illusion',
Is it a duck? A rabbit?
A duck-rabbit?
Hmmm . . .

What we see,
and how we see,
can be vastly different.
Making novel connections,
turning unfamiliar, abstract things,
into the familiar, distinctive and memorable,
is how we learn to see and interpret,
and shape things,
differently.

No Guarantee

Creativity,
has no guarantee.
Because something truly creative,
has never been done before.
It's a first.

There is no measure.
It's not proven. Not yet.
If creativity is in the business,
of producing novel ideas of value,
for human and cultural progress,
there is no guarantee,
on originality.

What We Have

We have,
all we need.
A sharp pencil,
and an imagination,
that likes to run,
wild.

Begin,
creating wonders.
Simply doodle away,
thoughts, ideas, curiosities.
We have to begin somewhere,
with what we have,
right here.

The Truth

The truth,
will set you free.
Be kind and brave,
with hidden and hard truths.
Give them oxygen to fly.
Lighten your load,
and enjoy life,
truthfully.

Creative Life Story

A creative life,
is an engaging story,
of curiosity, creativity and courage.
We may crave a little more something.
Dream big and imagine forward,
and take brave steps,
to go there.

Grumbling,
discontent is restless within us.
Listen carefully.
They're our hidden treasures,
calling us, waiting for us,
to find ways for them to surface,
and infiltrate our way of being,
to inspire and influence,
our creative life,
story.

The Problems We Encounter

Ego Rising

Our ego,
stands in the way,
of pathways to progress,
different perspectives.
Rise above,
that stubborn ego,
see the world above,
and beyond.

Miss Understood

Being,
misunderstood,
demonstrates that perception,
isn't always the reality.
I am not 'a suit'.
I am a *human being*,
Miss Understood,
with a creative heart,
of gold.

Pain And Possibility

Pain,
is a source of power,
waiting for us to make connections,
and build new pathways,
to possibility.

Inevitable Obstacles

Obstacles,
appear in many guises,
in the expansive landscape,
of a fulfilling creative life.
Accepting,
the inevitability of obstacles,
preserves some precious energy,
for viewing them as a necessary challenge,
testing our ability to overcome them,
making us stronger and more resilient,
to find new pathways forward.
Embrace life challenges,
with curiosity, creativity,
and courage.

ROX MARTYN

Fertile Failure

When we do,
brave creative things,
we will fail, over and over.
Without a doubt.
Our failures are essential.
They're building blocks,
for achieving,
greatness.

Festering Frustration

Frustrations,
fester away beneath,
the hard exterior we present,
hogging precious space,
for new thoughts to surface.
Release the pressure,
and let ideas,
flow.

Monsters And Mice

Our monsters,
appear when we're afraid,
rising from our hidden fears,
escaping through,
our voice.

Our mice,
retreat when we're afraid,
avoiding conflict and confrontations,
escaping from fears,
without a voice.

We live,
somewhere in between,
our big monsters and little mice,
where ugly monsters are controlled,
and little mice are encouraged,
making space for ourselves,
to find our own voice,
assert ourselves,
to be.

Fear Barrier

Skin,
thick or thin,
is always wrapped,
in a barrier,
of fear.
Meanwhile,
hidden beneath the surface,
our creative heart and un-lived life,
restlessly await a chance,
to escape the barrier,
and explore a world,
of creative living,
beyond fear.

Caging The Wild

When wild things,
become caged creatures,
watch their souls wither,
and the light inside,
slowly fade.

Dreams are lost,
wings clipped, creative muscle withers,
connection severed.
Paralysed and unable to fly,
to where the heart is aching to go,
without freedom to explore new pathways,
of a meaningful existence,
and essential growth.
The other side of the cage,
is a whole other,
story.

Carry Imposters

It sucks.
Every. Single. Time.
Without fail. Dammit. Here we go again.
When we are doing brave things,
nagging imposters appear.
Guaranteed.

'Hello there!'
They say, smugly.
Tapping us on the shoulder, annoyingly.
Knowing that we dread them.
But,
imposters are a good sign.
Because they are attracted to bravery.
Entertain their antics,
as they attempt to sabotage,
our creative progress,
Carry them on big adventures,
and say something like . . .
'Yep, I see you, imposter!
You had better be up for one hell of a ride,
because you and me,
we're going places,
my friend.'

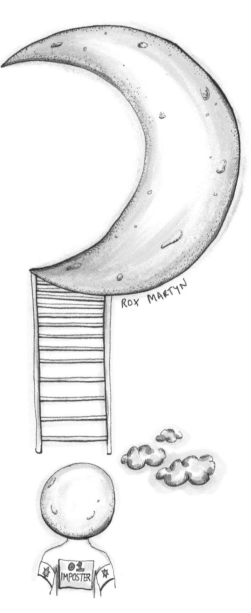

Our Shell

A shell,
is pretty handy,
as a protective home.
If you're a crustacean.
Not so great,
for hiding human beings.
Find a way out,
of our tempting shell.
Follow the light,
onto new pathways,
and possibilities,
in life.

Creating Boundaries

Boundaries,
preserve our integrity,
from soul-sucking thieves,
blocking unhelpful bombardments,
from entering into the atmosphere,
of our underserving minds.
We must protect our goodness,
and what matters to us,
from harsh words,
projected fears,
and lunatics.

Constant Distraction

Constant distraction,
is a sucker for creativity.
Just when we are getting into something,
our head deep into a world of ideas,
someone or something,
annoyingly snaps us back,
into stark reality.
Boom!
Ideas scatter,
a downward spin begins,
our chain of thought unravels,
thoughts drift and fade away.
And it's hard,
sometimes impossible,
to go back to where we were,
before.
Create space,
a little thought bubble,
to protect creative moments,
where nobody and nothing,
pulls us away from,
wanderings.

Opinions

Opinions,
are like buttholes,
we are all entitled to one,
and everyone has one.
Especially,
when it comes to creativity,
doing brave things,
and what matters,
to us.

Rock The Boat

Rock,
that boat, baby!
Please don't be afraid.
That boat needs to move,
to keep us on our toes.
Stand up,
with your voice,
shake the immovable,
make some waves,
and see where,
it goes.

The Multitasker

The Multitasker,
juggling and spinning,
around and around the clock,
in a whirl of 'important' stuff,
busy getting entangled,
in busyness.

Meanwhile,
wishing for another tentacle,
to tackle another menial task.
No 'me time' today.
Just dreaming,
of bed.

Queen Of Procrastination

Queen,
of Procrastination.
Avoids doing what must be done,
often mistaken for laziness,
but it's definitely not.
Promise!

Procrastination,
is our way of coping,
with challenging emotions,
anxiety, boredom, frustration,
and a whole heap of doubt,
to name a few.

Be curious,
notice what surfaces,
those unhelpful habits,
negative talk and emotions.
Let's not reward our brains,
with sweets and treats,
praising their avoidance,
behaviour.

Reward,
our troubled brains,
with a diet of better options.
Listen with curiosity and compassion,
to change the repeat pattern,
of procrastination.

Remove,
all tempting distractions,
lame excuses and roadblocks.
Paint a better picture,
of a tempting, rewarding outcome.
Make it an insightful game,
of self-discovery.

Can Do

Yes,
we can do hard things.
Step forward and begin to climb,
with vulnerability and courage.
Explore the wilderness.
Because 'I can't',
will take you,
nowhere.

Our Landscape Of Potential

Steps To Dreams

Dream big,
brave people.
Own those beauties.
Never let anyone steal them.
They are our precious beacons,
of hope and possibility,
to climb towards.
Step by step.
Every day.
We make progress,
with persistence and patience,
and consistent effort,
until we land.
The air is different,
up there.

Showing Up

Our life,
is our showtime.
Time to stand up and show up,
right here, right now.
Claim your power,
of curiosity, creativity and courage,
and show us the way,
forward.

Guiding Values

Lift,
your values high,
hold onto them nice and tight,
and let them guide you,
as you take,
flight.

Movement

People,
who move,
brains and bodies,
lead the way forward.
Creativity is movement,
going into unknown places,
with our wild imagination,
spinning the wheels,
of progress.

Creative Time

Tick tock,
says the clock,
waiting patiently,
for you to carve some,
wild and precious,
creative time.

Creative Practice

Commitment,
to our creative growth,
chipping away, every day,
is how we become better creators.
By putting in the emotional labour.
Pushing through the uncomfortable stuff,
until the failures outnumber the successes.
Then we know we're onto something.
Consistent and persistent practice,
of everyday creativity,
is how we make,
progress.

Helpful Habits

Okay,
so we want to become,
(more) creative.
Sounds like a fabulous idea.
But we haven't changed any habits,
to make this a possible,
new reality.

Small steps,
is how we go places in life.
By ditching old unhelpful habits,
and creating more helpful patterns,
we encourage our creativity,
to flow, connect and grow,
in a better direction.
Every. Single.
Day.

Naming Emotions

Emotions,
can lift us up,
or drag us down.
Brushed under the carpet,
they will inevitably surface,
escape and infiltrate,
our way of life.

And so,
we might entertain them,
by acknowledging and naming,
without judging or shaming,
and openly share them,
to normalise emotions,
and encourage,
others to join,
the party.

Empathy Shoes

Walk,
with curiosity,
in someone else's shoes.
Feel the raw pain of their reality,
of what it's like being them every day.
Only then can we truly know,
how to connect and engage,
our creative power,
to solve their problem,
and make life better,
somehow.

Head In The Clouds

Fluffy white clouds,
are magical for sticking your head into,
getting a whiff of fresh air.
It's very different,
up there.

A place,
to see clearly,
big dreams, distant lands,
somewhere to entertain wonder,
chase curiosity and wild ideas.
floating around alternative worlds,
playfully connecting.

A fresh perspective,
beyond our familiar world,
invigorates our creative heart.
Our feet planted firmly,
upon solid ground,
means no drifting away,
into the stratosphere.
(Not in the real world, anyway.)
So, go ahead,
stick your head up there,
into those clouds,
and dream,
away!

Living Practice

Hello!
I'm an artist.
When we do,
and proudly own,
what we say we do,
every day, we become.
Our creative practice,
shapes who we are,
what we make,
how we live,
and grow.

Our Heroes

We walk,
through life upon shoulders,
of giants and heroes.
We look up to them,
asking what they might do,
if they were you,
pondering the next,
move.

Meaningful Creation

A meaningful creation,
is something that matters to us,
and makes a difference.
It inspires, challenges and motivates us,
to endure the emotional labour,
of meaningful work,
as we create,
progress.

School Of Thought

Building,
and belonging to,
a school of thought,
within the field of creativity,
is a worthy cause and worldview,
a vision for the future,
our community,
of creators.

Play Away

Play away!
Let your imagination run wild,
go places and entertain new possibilities.
Bring joy, surprise and delight,
into our world.

As adults,
we claim not to have time,
for such indulgent 'useless frivolities'.
But play is essential for creativity,
and enjoying life in general.
Age doesn't matter.
Childlike wonder and play,
is timeless and keeps,
our creativity,
alive.

Snail Brain

Snail brain,
likes to dawdle,
to wonder and wander,
without nagging voices,
away from speedy distractions,
sniffing the fresh air,
soaking up *the good life,*
basking in nature,
letting thoughts surface,
and ruminate,
slowly.
In a relaxed state,
our minds open,
and exhale new thoughts.
Slow and precious,
is the value,
of time.

Goal Pathways

Big Goals,
are beacons of progress,
with myriad pathways to get there.
Step by step we climb hefty mountains,
overcoming challenges along the way.
Each pathway a learning curve,
unique experiences, interesting encounters,
fresh perspectives, alternative options,
insightful truths and hidden treasures.
Ensuring we reach our goal,
with a bucketload,
of fulfilment.

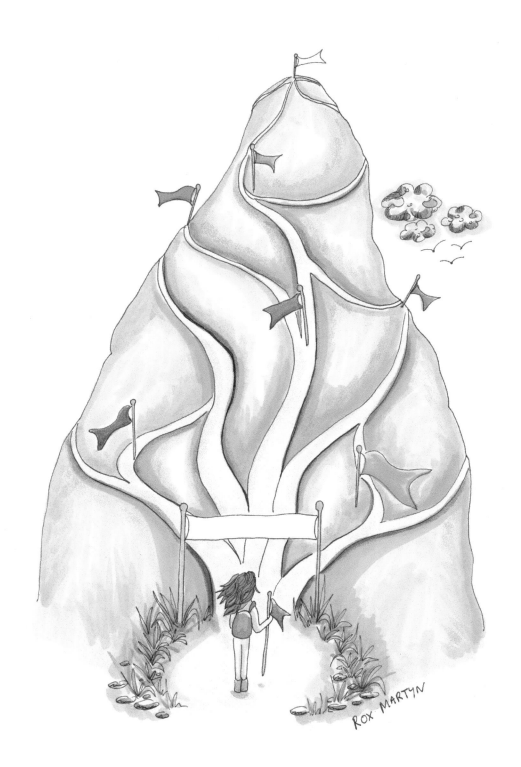

Audacious Goals

A goal,
worth chasing,
is slightly out of reach.
Not too close, not too far.
One small step for us,
is a giant leap,
forward.

Intrinsic Reward

Flashy fame,
and sparkly awards,
might seem rather glamorous.
But what matters more,
is the reward we feel *within* us,
when our hidden treasures glow,
and our creative heart feels alive,
in celebration of our achievements.
The real measure of success in life,
our most meaningful reward,
is what radiates proudly,
from *within*.

Cultivating Relationships

Relationships,
are cultivated,
by human connection.
We may not see eye to eye,
our minds may not think alike,
but we bond over what matters.
Connected we do better,
and go places,
together.

Life Dreams

Life,
becomes enriched,
by chasing big, wild dreams.
The things we dream of doing,
places we dream of going,
people we dream of,
becoming.

Human achievement,
begins with a big dream in life,
and embarking upon adventures,
to explore all sorts of ways,
of making our dreams,
come true.

Colourful Personality

Absorb,
appreciate and admire,
the wonderful spectrum of colour,
the magic and magnitude,
of being a whole human,
with many facets,
of intriguing,
personality.

Identity Picture

Our identity,
grows from within,
and the connections we make,
within the enchanting world around us.
We are much more than ourselves.
We are an evolving painting,
of our complete,
picture.

ROX MARTYN

Our Creative Identity

Our identity,
is there for us to shape,
and develop fully.
With inquisitive introspection,
and by chasing our curiosity,
we discover our creative power,
and human potential.
Shall we?
Spread our wings,
and embark upon adventures,
around landscapes and faraway lands,
to explore a whole world,
of possibility.

CHAPTER THREE

The Realm Of Discovery

This chapter explores **the bigger picture** and **contextual landscape** to discover **interesting problems** and opportunities to make a difference. It seeks to entice you beyond your comfort zones and into the unknown to gather insights and inspiration to make novel connections and seed bright ideas.

Navigate the **Realm Of Discovery** and explore:

* Where novel ideas come from.
* What happens when we chase our curiosity.
* The power of connection making.
* Common barriers to creative discovery.
* A spectrum of ways to inspire different thinking and novel ideas.

Because, when we know our contextual landscape better, we open our world to a whole treasure chest of golden nuggets for our creaitvity to feast upon.

Our World Beyond

Our Bigger Picture

See beyond,
expected familiarity.
Soak up what lies beyond,
our comfort and chase curiosity.
Scan the beauty of a bigger picture.
Experience a different perspective.
The enriching landscape of life,
is where creativity thrives.
Our canvas to make,
a glowing impact.
One small step,
at a time.

The Explorer

The explorer,
embarks upon big adventures.
with wide eyes, an open mind,
and a wild imagination,
inhaling an unknown world beyond,
playing with the seeds of novel ideas,
discovering interesting truths,
navigating unexpected challenges.
This is how we engage with the world,
on a quest to become,
braver and better,
Creators.

Dancing With Fear

Fear,
can be a mighty force,
blocking us from doing brave things.
But it needn't be this way.
Diminish its daunting power,
loosen its persistent grasp,
and dance with fears.
Give them air time,
lighten the load,
and go places,
together.

Comfort Zones

Hiding away,
in our familiar comfort zones,
a spectator to the unfolding reality beyond,
withdrawn from the ambiguity of life,
prevents us from engaging,
with the world.

To make an impact,
step outside the comfort zone,
explore new landscapes further afield,
expanding horizons of possibility,
uncovering interesting truths,
and a meaningful purpose,
for progress to happen,
beyond comfort.

Curiosity Compass

Curiosity,
nudges us forward.
It's our magnet for movement,
for inspiring creative progress.
By following our curiosity compass,
engaging our sense of wonder,
we travel bravely into the unknown,
where creativity comes alive,
with its marvellous magic,
teetering on the edge,
of possibility.

Time Capsule

It's time,
to buckle up, buttercup,
switch on that imagination,
power up your engine,
travel into the past,
maybe the future,
and discover,
a different,
reality.

Mind Wandering

Mind Wandering,
is often frowned upon.
We've been trained to conform,
to control our minds, stay focused,
not to wander off the usual beaten track.
But this is damaging for our creativity,
which surfaces precisely when,
our minds wander.
Meander through nature,
give your mind permission to wonder,
play with new connections.
The fruitful wanderings,
that seed ideas.

Different Pathways

'One way'
isn't an option.
If we seek different,
and better ways forward,
there are many options,
to explore, connect and grow,
beyond our familiar world,
into unknown landscapes,
of creative possibility.

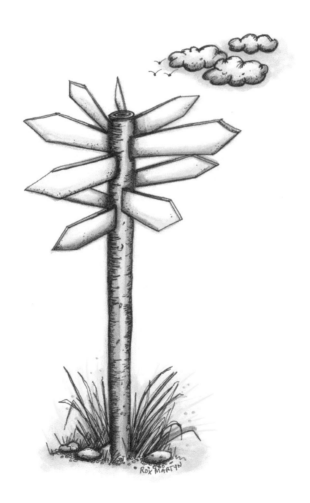

Catching Ideas

Every day,
ideas hover quietly,
sometimes unnoticeable,
to our naked human eye,
lurking beneath the radar.
These buzzing little ideas,
might hold the power,
and potential,
to change,
life.

Pattern Making

Explore,
beyond and further afield.
Cross boundaries into new territories.
Expand horizons, clear ground and make space.
Be curious about the patterns that arise.
Dissect and decipher,
what's helpful and unhelpful.
Choose a pattern to work with,
to build upon, or change.
Make a better pattern,
and then bring it,
to life.

Collecting Things

Observant collectors,
gather things seemingly useless.
An ever-growing collection of curiosities,
of weird and wonderful treasures.
A tactile pebble. A rusty coin.
Beads, buttons and bugs.
A feather, or two.
An evacuated shell.
Broken glass, washed smooth.
Just because.
Who knows what and where,
our next big idea,
will grow from.

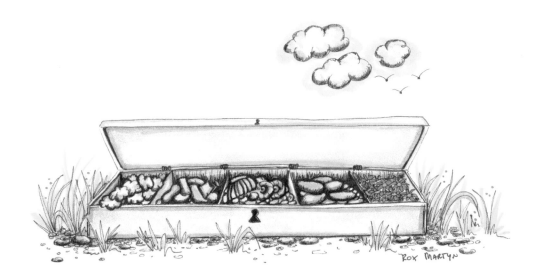

Pool Of Inspiration

Inspiration,
can be found everywhere,
if we open our minds,
and switch on our radar,
to receive what lurks,
out there.

To feel inspired,
be inspiring to others,
and make inspiring things happen,
we must become inspired ourselves,
and cultivate our pool,
of inspiration.

Note Worthy

Sometimes,
the simplest tools,
like a notebook and pen,
are the most effective,
most trusted companions,
to carry with us,
on our travels.
Hovering,
waiting to capture,
our thoughts and observations,
to record what sparks,
something worth,
noting.

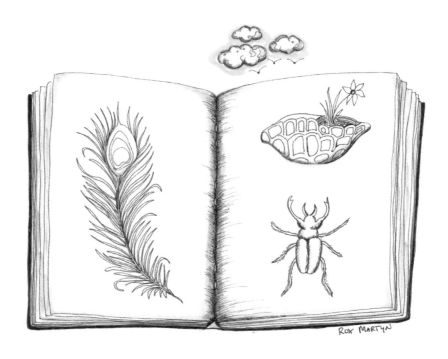

Rules Of The Road

Creativity,
comes out to play,
when it feels safe to do so,
without judgement or criticism,
the weight of negative vibes,
where it's free to explore,
to entertain bold ideas.
So make some rules,
for creativity,
to make,
magic.

The Problems We Encounter

Middle Ground

Middle Ground,
is the place between,
off the radar and into the ether,
and sticking to where you are,
going nowhere.

Sometimes,
creativity gets us lost off radar,
which can reveal hidden treasures,
but the trick is knowing,
when to return to the fertile,
Middle Ground.

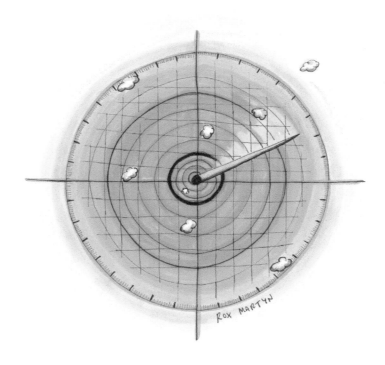

Lost Wonder

Wonder,
gets lost in enchanted woods,
of our childhood.
Far away from our thoughts,
as mundane duties of adulthood take over.
But without our childlike wonder,
our wild imagination withers away,
with no wonder to play,
and entertain our curiosity.
Our big dreams and wild ideas,
secret worlds and adventures,
our magical creativity,
desperately needs,
to find our lost,
wonder.

Unknown Territory

Unknown territory,
might be hiding our golden key,
to open new realms into the future.
A little darkness and discomfort,
risk and uncertainty,
might be worth,
a big gain.

Mountains And Molehills

Our brains,
are wired for creativity.
Which means they have a tendency,
to be rather creative with the truth,
imaginatively inventing the worst.
Molehills become mountains,
in the world of creativity.
Putting up roadblocks,
if we let them,
hijack our,
way.

Avoiding Tension

It's tempting,
to see tension and conflict brewing,
and run for the hills to hide out.
But if we learn to see differently,
the canyons of tension become insightful,
uncovering buried truths and treasures,
fears and festering frustration,
unmet needs, wants, desires,
insecurities and anxieties.
All of these, and more,
are valuable clues bubbling away,
sparking curiosity, conversation,
cultivating bright ideas,
that inspire change,
for the better.

Navigating Challenges

Our choice,
whether to accept,
the challenges of life with grace,
to navigate them, learn, move forward,
and persist with our adventures of discovery.
Or turn back, empty-handed,
and begin again,
someday.
Maybe.

Important Problems

We live,
in a world of problems,
within the landscape of life.
Some are screaming for attention,
others, whispering gently.
Waiting. Waiting. Waiting.
For us to notice and do something,
to step forward with courage.
Embrace the problem,
that matters,
most.

Lighten Up

Negativity,
is a heavy burden.
Negative voices,
swirl around and around,
persistently attempting to chuck,
our creative power,
overboard.

Our narrative,
can drag us down.
So dump it overboard.
Good riddance!
Enjoy heady heights,
of a lighter cognitive load,
and embark upon brave adventures,
with exhilarating, uplifting,
thoughts.

Lurking Trolls

The brave,
cross bridges into unknown territory,
to discover new, fertile ground,
beyond familiar lands,
to expand the landscape of possibility,
and go places in life.
Beware of lurking trolls,
waiting to pounce,
seeking to throw the brave off track,
sometimes over the bridge,
because they know,
no better than,
down below.

Our Landscape Of Opportunity

Going There

Creativity,
feeds on inspiration,
insightful sensory experiences,
gathering valuable information,
extracting golden insights,
from unfamiliar worlds.
By going there,
we uncover,
wonders.

Random Connections

Creativity,
changes the way we see,
and engage with the world.
When we train our brain,
to see differently,
we make interesting connections,
and playful combinations.
Entertain creativity in everyday life.
Exercise, stretch and build,
that powerful creative muscle,
by simply wandering through nature,
away from the glare of screens,
to see a magical world,
beyond.

Away With The Fairies

Away,
with the fairies,
is an enchanting place to be.
The tricky bit is knowing,
when to call it a day,
and return back to reality,
with golden nuggets,
for our creativity,
to feast upon.

Rabbit Holes

Chasing,
our nagging curiosity,
down winding rabbit holes,
researching, poking and prodding,
churning the soil, digging for truths,
down deep beneath the surface,
where the real treasure,
glows in darkness.

Observation

Observation,
of our surroundings,
reveals the intricacies of life.
Noticing and noting what we see,
transporting information and thoughts,
from head to hand, and onto paper,
filtered through our unique,
creative lens, we create,
our masterpiece.

Idea Seeds

Catch them!
Quickly while you can.
Floating aimlessly in the breeze.
They are the seeds of ideas,
sprinkling a little magic,
new beginnings,
into life.

Hidden Doors

Hidden doors,
are everywhere, if we look.
Secret portals into another world,
waiting for us to step forward.
Open, peek and explore,
the beauty beyond,
the known.
Into the unknown,
where opportunities live,
within an expansive horizon,
an enchanting landscape.
Where new pathways,
slowly unfurl.

Golden Nuggets

Entangled in chaos,
nestled in layers of complexity,
and often slightly out of reach,
are golden nuggets of insight.
The inspiration we seek,
to spark conversation,
feed our creativity,
gain strength,
learn, grow,
and,
fly.

Campfire Stories

Our travels,
expand our world,
in so many wonderful ways.
The interesting people we meet,
and different places we go,
reveal something unique.
Adventures, struggles, successes,
tales of bravery and vulnerability,
captivating stories enthusiastically shared,
around the comforting glow of the campfire.
Here we transform our perspective,
beyond our familiar reality,
igniting our curiosity,
kindling connection,
for our untold,
unfolding,
story.

Envisioning

Thinking forward,
envisioning alternative worlds,
is rather entertaining and enlightening.
Imagine if we had a crystal ball,
we could stick our head right into it,
catch a glimpse of what life might be like,
how things might be different,
the secrets of the unseen world of the future.
And then begin, step by step,
to bridge the gap with bright ideas,
inching us towards the change,
we seek to make.

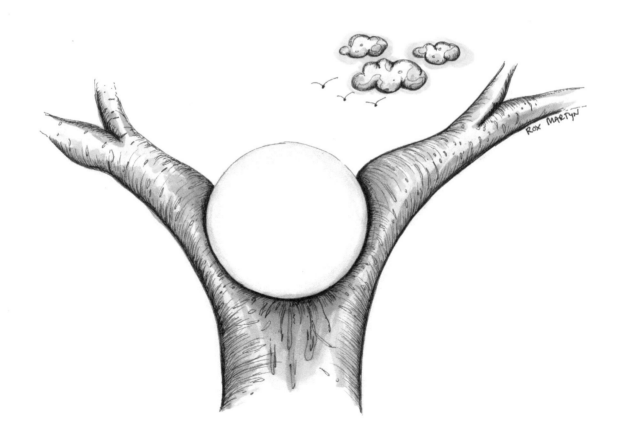

Better Questions

'Stop asking questions.'
We might hear this, many times over.
But *better questions* are a gateway,
to a world of insightful discovery.
Why. How. What. Who. When. Where.
In search of meaningful truths,
that light our pathway,
forward.

Unexpected Encounters

Encounters,
fall unexpectedly in life,
randomly landing on our pathway.
In the realms of creativity,
anything is possible.

Be open,
and highly curious,
about what comes your way.
It might just be the little seeds,
that grow into something,
much bigger, like,
Velcro!

Little Delights

Nature,
our enchanting world,
of small pleasures,
little delights,
with their timeless fascination,
generation after generation.
Small yet mighty,
stopping us in our tracks,
sparking wonder, chasing curiosity,
cherished moments in time,
when the clock pauses,
and we rise high,
upon the winds of nature,
into magical realms,
of possibility.

Seeing Connections

Our world,
is a wonderland of connection,
for creativity.
We look and see, pause and reflect,
play until our creative hearts' content,
entertaining our wildest dreams,
chasing our child-like curiosity,
to the edges of our imagination,
building novel connections.
Everyone belongs here,
in our wonderland,
making magic,
happen.

Above And Below

Hidden,
beneath the tip of the iceberg,
is a mysterious and vast underworld,
of restless thoughts and hard truths,
where precious insights lurk,
beneath the surface.

Search,
above and below,
to discover lost and buried treasures,
and the hidden seeds,
of bright ideas.

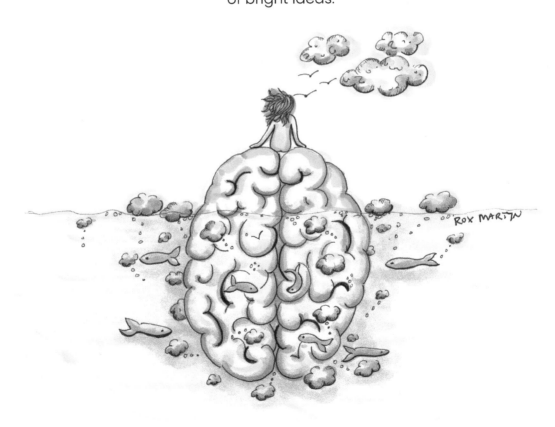

Insightful Discovery

Dig deep,
much deeper,
beneath the surface,
where ancient clues hide.
Unearth the lost treasures of life,
a rare and insightful discovery,
enlightens us with,
new truths.

Mysterious Things

We wonder,
about the big mysteries in life.
The universe, the planets, the stars.
But the little mysteries are powerful too,
like bugs, bees and blades of grass,
things too small for the eye to see.
Mysterious forces of our world,
like magnetism and gravity.
The mighty small things,
lead to our greatest,
discoveries.

Myths And Mysteries

Our lives,
are enriched and inspired,
by ancient treasures.
Myths and mysteries of the past,
mythical creatures,
legendary tales,
gift us with curiosities to chase,
spark our imagination,
entertain weird and wild possibilities,
unexpected connections,
between past, present and future,
opening alternative worlds,
of possibility to explore,
a new and unfolding,
creative life,
story.

Creative Opportunity

Creative opportunity,
lives within the gaping void,
between our stark reality and our distant dreams,
where persistent tension,
and festering frustration,
wait patiently,
for curiosity, creativity and courage,
to build a bridge,
forward.

CHAPTER FOUR
The Realm Of Creation

This chapter encourages the exploration of **purposeful challenges** and **creative possibilities** to inspire bright ideas and meaningful creations. It seeks to expand your thinking to go beyond the default, safe and easy, nudging you into unknown territory and towards the edges of possibility.

Navigate the **Realm Of Creation** and explore:

* Why a purposeful challenge matters.
* How bright ideas become meaningful creations.
* What enables creativity to shine and make an impact.
* Common barriers to creative possibility.
* Ways of enticing brave ideas to surface.

Because, when we know what the creative possibilities are, where the edges are, and where the connection happens, we make space to cultivate bright ideas into meaningful creations.

Our World Of Creation

The Creator

The creator,
inspires and influences,
how we live and progress in life.
With a big vision and bright ideas,
they imagine a better world,
and carve pathways,
to take us there.

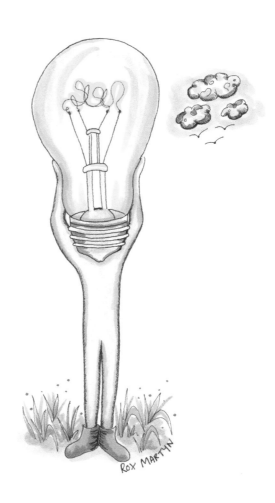

Everyday Problems

Observing,
with patient curiosity,
might spark a connection,
strike a chord, a little compassion,
for people and problems,
worth solving.

Shared Purpose

People,
work better together,
bonded by a shared purpose,
something meaningful to everyone.
Our creative dynamic,
delivers diverse and distinctive,
creative contribution,
with purpose.

Purposeful Challenge

A problem,
one worth solving,
becomes a purposeful challenge,
when it inspires us to make,
something useful,
and become masters,
of our best work,
yet.

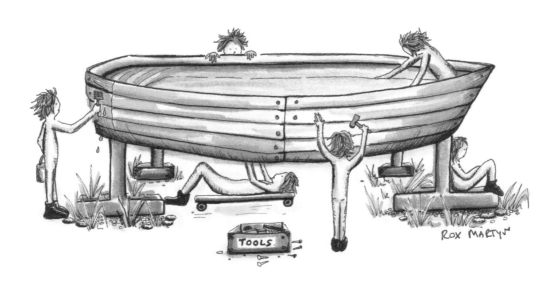

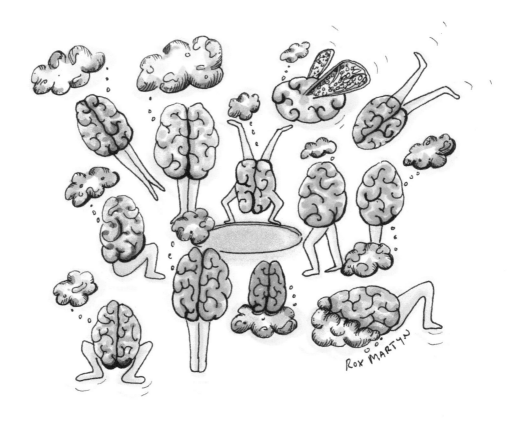

Great Minds

Great minds,
don't always think alike.
So shake it up!
With different thinking,
a dynamic bunch of playful minds,
blending and bumping,
chilling, flying and diving,
throwing diverse ideas,
into thin air.
Step back and curiously watch,
the mighty mind magic,
create wonders.

Challenging Assumptions

Sometime,
a long time ago,
allegedly, people thought,
the world was flat.
Imagine that!

By challenging,
our adopted assumptions,
and things we take for granted,
we are liberated to explore beyond.
Asking different questions,
probing for new truths,
is how we discover,
a new reality.

Collaborative Creativity

Creative,
collaborative worker bees,
each pulling their share of weight,
for a common purpose, a greater good.
Contributing in their own distinctive way,
chucking ideas into one big melting pot.
Bubbling, blending and becoming,
a potent, creative potion,
of possibility.

Spectrum Of Contribution

A spectrum,
of creative contribution,
comes from diverse directions,
different cultures, minds, perspectives, expertise,
a powerful concoction of creative energy,
blending, brewing and becoming,
a pool of bright ideas.

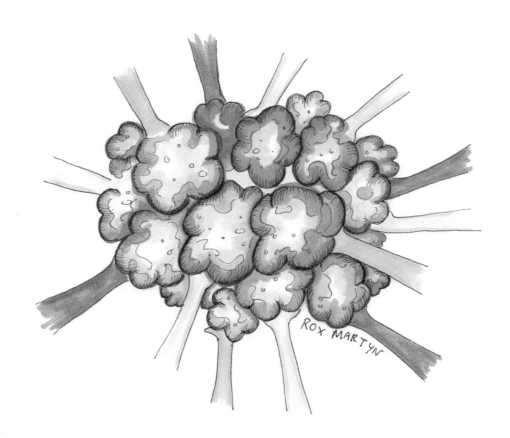

Conscious Creativity

Our planet,
is mighty enormous,
but also mighty precious.
Human actions,
have caused significant damage,
irreparable and irreversible,
harm.

SOS,
calling all humans,
with an ounce of conscience.
We need collective creativity,
with good purpose.
Step forward,
with curiosity, creativity and courage.
Do something to protect,
our mighty precious,
beautiful home,
Planet Earth.

Time Flies

Time flies,
when we're having fun,
working on purposeful challenges.
Losing all track of time,
is a telling sign,
of creativity,
at work.

Powerful Intuition

The origins,
seeds of bright ideas,
evolve from human insight,
made possible by a trio of lenses.
Curiosity, Empathy and Imagination.
This powerful human intersection,
our intuitive lens on life,
enables us to create,
wonders.

Effort And Reward

Effort matters.
We need to put in the effort,
to gain the reward.
Expecting the prize,
without putting in the effort,
simply becomes ugly,
entitlement.
The more ideas we make,
the higher the chance,
of enjoying better,
rewards.

Seeing Patterns

Look out,
watch and see,
interesting patterns,
unfurling, becoming,
a new way of life,
for you and,
me.

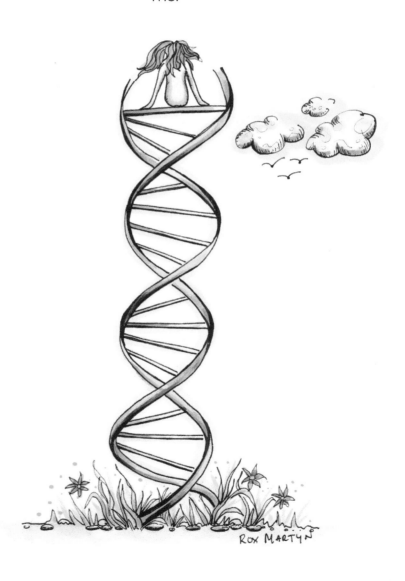

The Problems We Encounter

Rejection Pile

The computer says 'no'.
An effortless, automated response overrides,
anything that breaks the system,
the pattern of the norm,
daring to deviate from the standard,
the predictable,
disrupting the smooth flow,
of the conveyor belt.

Human rejection,
doesn't make our work bad,
it just might not fit the system.
Wrong time, wrong person,
maybe having a bad day.
All things beyond,
our control.

Belief,
and unbreakable persistence,
practising, learning and improving,
building upon a pile of rejection,
is how our work evolves,
and eventually gets,
accepted.

Idea Hoarding

Stand up,
get off your butt,
stop hoarding those ideas.
The world needs your creativity,
to rise way above the surface,
make new connections,
solve problems, discover possibilities,
and show us a better way,
of being.

Setting Expectations

Expectations,
are tricky things.
Sometimes too high or too low,
spoken, unspoken, conscious, unconscious,
unrealistic, unreasonable, unfair,
they're lurking somewhere.
What we hope for, and what we get,
might be two worlds,
apart.

Fear Of Originality

Dear Originality,
you're driving me nuts.
I feel you breathing down my neck,
and fear you circling around my ideas.
This reminds me of something.
It's already been done.
You're not creative.
You repeatedly,
bang on.

But,
you clearly fail to see,
this hasn't been done before.
Not by me, through my eyes,
using my unique lens on life,
exploring different angles,
giving familiar ideas,
my magic spin.

And so,
Dear Originality,
I refuse to entertain you.
As of today, without regret,
you're fired, with immediate effect.
I'm replacing you with something more useful,
for cultivating creativity and bright ideas,
encouraging unique contributions.
From my creative heart,
please welcome,
Authenticity.

Vicious Circles

Creativity,
has an absolute blast,
going around and around in circles.
But vicious circles are nauseating,
and also mildly torturous.
Going nowhere fast.
Until we break the pattern,
and fly with focus,
forward.

Beware Biases

Beware of biases.
They come in many disguises,
lurking everywhere, within everyone,
waiting for a chance to pounce,
upon our bright ideas.
Catch them in action at work.
Name and frame them.
Prevent them from distorting,
perspectives and decisions,
our efforts to make,
good progress.

Wandering Into Focus

Creativity,
loves to wander off track,
diverting our attention away from focus,
entertaining all sorts of distractions,
sprinkling sweets along unknown pathways,
tempting us further astray.
But when we bring our creativity home,
concentrate its magical power,
we blend, build and create,
focused wonders.

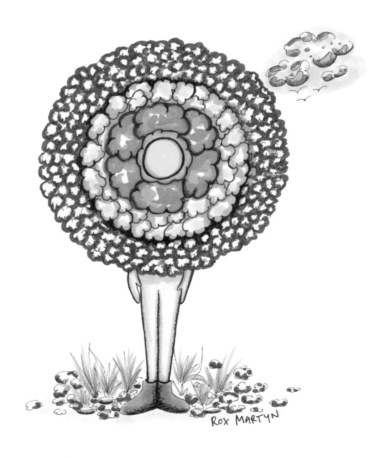

Parking Judgement

Judgement,
blocks our creative pathways,
preventing new and brave ideas,
from entering into the mix.
Crushing the seeds of bright ideas,
before they've even seen daylight,
without a chance to take flight.
Liberated from destructive judgement,
ideas can explore their potential,
show us a different direction,
nudge us into new territory,
change our perspective,
and make unexpected,
possibilities,
happen.

Idea Crushers

Bold ideas,
the kind that are risky,
open new doors and lead change,
seem to attract clumsy fools,
with a dislike for novelty.
The change resisters,
have big feet,
that crush,
possibility.

Start Stop

Start,
and just when you're on a roll,
in the thick of things,
stop.

Start, again,
and just when you're getting back into it,
finding where you left off,
stop.

Repeat,
until your head explodes,
with frustration.

Constant interruptions,
disrupt the flow,
of creativity.

Objectivity And Subjectivity

Creativity,
retreats, disconnects and withers,
when closed to possibility,
with subjectivity,
and scrutiny.

I can't put my finger on it,
I just don't like it,
My grandma's dog was called that,
This reminds me of something,
It looks weird.

Creativity,
roams, connects and grows,
when open to possibility,
with objectivity,
and praise.

I see this has potential,
I'm open to being convinced,
Let's explore further,
I'm curious to know where this goes,
What if we . . .

Negativity Spirals

Creativity,
is a powerful force of change.
A curious, exploratory and positive practice,
drawn into the heights of new realms,
where wild imaginations roam.
But easily entangled,
and quickly dragged down,
into downward spirals,
of negativity.

Notice,
negativity at work,
dragging our creative efforts down,
stalling us from going places,
unexpected and different.
The change resisters,
fear novelty and unpredictability,
preferring the expected,
sticking to safety in the familiar.
Stay strong, stand proud,
speak up, step around,
and move onwards,
and upwards.

Under Pressure

Creativity,
under pressure,
can be good, bad and very ugly.
Too little pressure,
and it wanders endlessly.
Too much pressure,
and it becomes paralysed.
But when the pressure,
is like Goldilocks' porridge,
ahhh, just right,
our creativity,
feasts and,
flows.

Criticism

Criticism,
suffocates creativity.
Before mouths open wide,
ready to exhale toxic words,
quickly engage the boundaries,
protect our souls from impact,
and block harsh criticism,
from striking,
people.

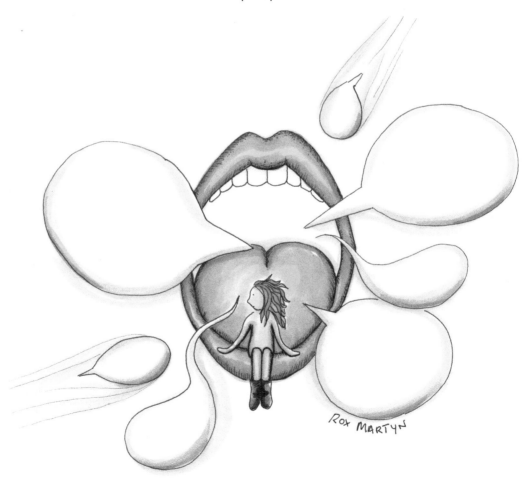

Helpful Feedback

Feedback,
easily offends people,
and derails our creativity.
It might not intend to be that way,
so take the time and make the effort,
to consider and filter your thoughts.
Craft a more helpful response.
Choose words carefully.
Clear and kind,
every time.

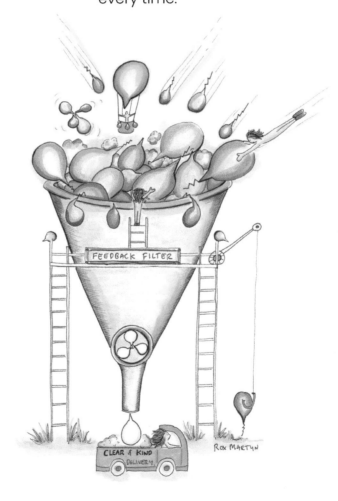

Good Enough

Perfectionism,
when we live in an imperfect world,
inhabited by imperfect people,
with imperfect conditions and circumstances,
isn't realistic or attainable.
It's rather painful.
By relaxing our expectations a little,
we choose to make progress,
over pointless, perpetual perfectionism,
and become willing to accept,
that what matters most,
is good enough.

Polishing Turds

A turd,
is a turd, my love.
No matter how much you tweak,
polish and decorate.
It will always be,
a turd.

Drawing The Line

Creativity,
always wants to do more,
dreaming, tinkering,
procrastinating,
preening.
Any excuse to avoid,
doing what must be done.
Drawing the line.
Setting our bright ideas free,
to fly into the world,
inspire change,
and grow.

Our Landscape Of Creative Possibility

Framing Challenges

Problems,
become interesting,
purposeful challenges,
viewed from different directions,
and skilfully framed.
Hidden problems, truths, needs, wants,
brought to the surface,
framed as questions to be explored.
Envisioning the impact,
we seek to make.
Expanding the horizons of possibility,
an inspiring contextual landscape,
for bright ideas to grow.
With boundaries, constraints and considerations,
the whole picture frames,
our challenge.

Idea Peacock

Idea Peacock,
gracefully opens,
and expands our imagination,
fanning a wonderful spectrum,
of unexpected creative possibility,
embracing the weird and wonderful,
connecting and cultivating,
bright ideas into,
something,
magical.

Powerful Truths

Bright ideas,
grow from powerful truths,
little golden nuggets of inspiration,
giving purpose and power to our creativity.
And with a little imagination,
a truth simply expressed,
makes our creations,
impactful.

Unlikely Pairings

Watch out,
for unlikely pairs.
They do surprising things.
An interesting contrast of experience,
paradox and juxtaposition,
challenge the norm, expand our edges,
nudge us to think beyond,
the expected.

Organising Ideas

Creativity,
has a tendency for chaos,
but we can learn to organise our ideas.
Gathering input from an expansive picture,
into one big pot of bubbling bright ideas,
decide upon a sorting criteria,
and organise them,
into action.

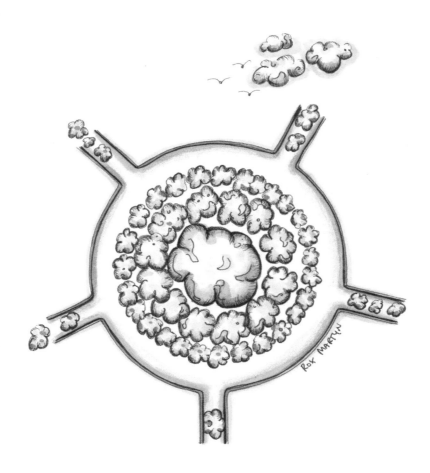

Idea Weaving

Bright ideas,
become meaningful creations,
when cultivated,
and woven together,
to tell a complete story,
of a changed,
world.

Sleeping On It

Creativity,
and everyone,
has a unique rhythm.
Working magic around the clock,
sometimes charging around in the open,
other times contemplating slowly beneath the surface.
Our distinctive, individual creative rhythm,
enables powerful magic to happen.
Notice what we really need,
move to that rhythm,
and be creative,
beings.

Tree Hugging

Hugging trees,
like a sleepy sloth,
is completely underrated,
and sometimes gets a bad wrap.
But honestly, it's worth giving it a go.
It does wonders for our creativity.
Feel the warm pulse of nature,
seeping through layers,
touching our heart,
as we hug,
our tree.

Clever Improvisation

Improvisation,
is creativity on fire.
On the spot, no time to dither,
no fancy resources, magic tools or script.
And with not much to work with,
we create something,
wonderful.

Simplifying Complexity

Complexity,
can cause havoc and run riot,
overwhelming our lives,
if left to fester and grow,
unattended.
Mastering the art of simplicity,
is a valuable skill in life.
Taking conscious effort and time,
to understand complex matters,
edit and craft them,
into something easily grasped,
simply becomes more,
useful.

Playful Juxtaposition

Creativity,
plays with juxtaposition,
connecting, entertaining, imagining,
unlikely combinations.
Matchmaking,
delicate flower fairies,
with powerful fast cars.
seemingly polar opposites,
but together they create wonders,
with interesting stories,
waiting to be,
told.

Alternative Uses

We have,
so many things in our lives,
there's something for everything,
and an abundance of alternatives for something.
We can be creative in many wonderful ways,
and make a little magic,
from everyday,
things.

Beautiful Constraint

Constraints,
give creativity some edges,
to grow wonders within,
a place to cultivate its power.
Without constraint,
creativity wanders over the horizon,
endlessly meandering and exploring.
Creativity needs constraint,
a safe place to grow,
into something,
bigger.

Little Experiments

Our ecosystem,
the contextual landscape of life,
is a wonderful place,
to conduct little experiments,
on our novel ideas.
Somewhere we feel safe to try,
and fail, repeatedly.
To push our ideas into play,
set sail, test the waters.
To observe, learn and improve,
over and over again.
Until something,
eventually,
floats.

Evaluating Ideas

Bright ideas,
need to be carefully evaluated,
for their relevance, value and usefulness,
in the real world.
Bright ideas,
have the power and potential,
to make an impact,
small, big, or somewhere in between,
for some people, somewhere.
Somehow influencing,
life changes.
The clue,
is not missing a clue,
failing to notice,
what makes or breaks,
bright ideas.

Provocation

Things,
are rarely a given.
People, concepts, ideas, products,
anything else that matters to us,
they're all a work in progress.
Anything worthwhile in life,
only becomes better,
with purposeful,
provocation.

Elaboration

People,
and the seeds of ideas,
have lots of delightful things,
in common.
We grow in the right environment,
ground beneath, oxygen around, sunlight above.
With a little nudge and nurturing,
we gain confidence to explore,
with curiosity, creativity and courage,
to weave an elaborate story,
together.

Meaningful Creation

Bright ideas,
cultivated into reality,
become meaningful creations,
when accepted and adopted in everyday life.
Changing our landscape for the better,
bringing us closer together,
becoming a better,
way of life,
forever.

Persuasive Presentation

A bright idea,
falls flat on its face,
before a bemused audience,
in the eerie absence,
of a deep and meaningful connection.
Hitting a nerve, striking a chord, exposing a truth,
building a contextual story of relevance,
is how we inspire change and progress.
When our audience becomes engaged,
listening intently and curiously,
becoming part of the story,
we bring them with us,
along for the ride.
This is *our story*,
our persuasive,
presentation.

Creative Mastery

Practise,
doesn't make perfect,
it patiently develops our mastery,
when we choose something,
that matters to us,
and extends our reach,
beyond comfort.
A meaningful purpose,
becomes a passion, a labour of love,
enthusiastically embraced every day,
chipping away, persistently and
consistently,
word by word, block by block,
building something special,
with our creative power,
to become masters,
of what we do.

CHAPTER FIVE

The Realm Of Progress

This chapter inspires **creative progress**, for brave ideas to become a new and meaningful way of life. It seeks to encourage you to integrate creativity into everyday business and champion the way forward.

Navigate the **Realm Of Progress** and explore:

* Why creativity needs catalysts to move forward.
* How to orchestrate and cultivate creativity to make bright ideas happen.
* Business and creativity working better together.
* Common barriers to creative progress.
* Paving the way forward with curiosity, creativity and courage.

Because, when we know how creativity becomes effective in sparking change, we can make better choices to keep the wheels in motion.

Our World Of
Creative Champions

Creative Leaders

Creativity,
needs brave leadership,
creative leaders with a big vision,
an imagination to envision the future,
painting an enticing picture of change,
the success story we hope for.
And then make pathways,
to get there.

Creative leaders,
gather people for the ride,
each willingly pulling their weight,
contributing in their own way,
en route to a greater good.
Championing bright ideas,
moving us all forward,
with their curiosity,
creativity and,
courage.

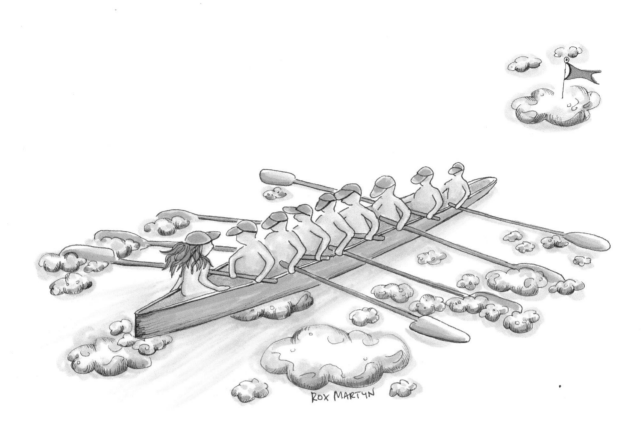

Clear Vision

A clear vision,
is a beacon for progress,
something meaningful to strive for.
A place of hope where big dreams land,
nudging us gently into a new reality.
Pushing on through all troublesome encounters,
with curiosity, creativity and courage.
The blood, sweat and tears,
build our resilience, make us stronger,
stretching us beyond comfort,
to lean into and land,
upon our vision.

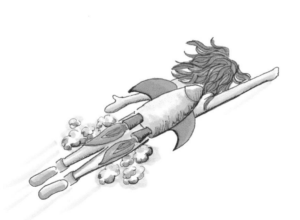

Champions Of Creativity

Together,
we make progress,
as champions of creativity.
Each making a small bridge,
becoming a connective structure.
One by one. Brick by brick. Step by step.
Weaving our valuable contributions together,
bridging the gap between worlds apart,
making something bigger than us.
A new pathway clears the way,
for bright ideas to travel,
and lead us into,
the future.

Influential Ideas

Bright ideas,
need to partner with influence,
to propel them forward,
braving the winds of change,
stirring the air, ripples of progress,
is how we land with impact,
to shift the landscape,
and create a world,
of change.

Real Productivity

Productivity,
isn't how fast we go,
how much we do, how late we stay,
how many things we stuff,
into our day.

Real productivity,
is the difference we make,
the change, progress and impact,
of our unique creative power at work,
persistently and consistently,
cultivating novel ideas.
The difference being,
what matters.

Roles And Responsibilities

Roles,
play to our strengths,
enabling us to branch out and explore,
our potential and possibilities,
and contribution within,
the parameters,
of our role.

Responsibilities,
hold us accountable to a purpose,
with things we need to action,
our commitment,
to achieve.

To conquer,
big hairy audacious goals,
complex problems and challenges,
we need clearly defined and adopted,
roles and responsibilities.
Because we do better,
and go further,
working better,
together.

Bridging Gaps

Opportunity,
lives in unexpected places.
Deep canyons of tension,
unbridged lands and gaping voids.
Perfect places for festering frustration,
and brewing problems.
Waiting, patiently,
for a little pressure to be released,
powerful connections to be made.
A bridge over troubled waters,
becomes a platform to see,
change on the horizon,
and a better way,
forward.

Human Progress

Bright ideas,
are like bouncy springs,
they enable us to move forward.
Our little inventions,
are springboards for giant leaps,
launching us into a world,
of novel possibilities,
to change our way of life,
inspire and influence,
human progress.

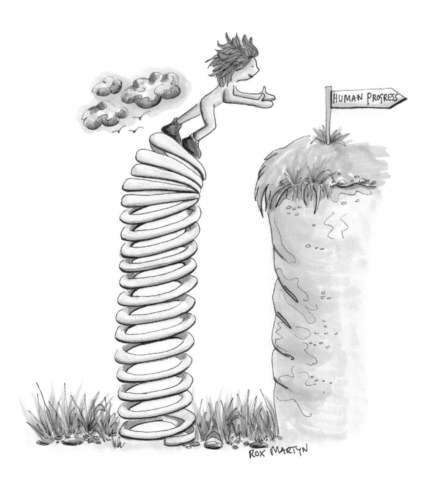

Walk The Talk

Our words,
belong alongside our actions,
walking and talking,
chattering away happily together.
When we are doing,
what we say,
people will look and listen,
as we walk and talk,
and show them,
the way.

Integrating Creativity

'Creativity upstream',
isn't good enough today,
it needs to become,
the vibrant beating heart,
of human beings, organisations and culture,
integrated within,
embracing the whole picture,
infiltrating the veins,
of our creative,
existence.

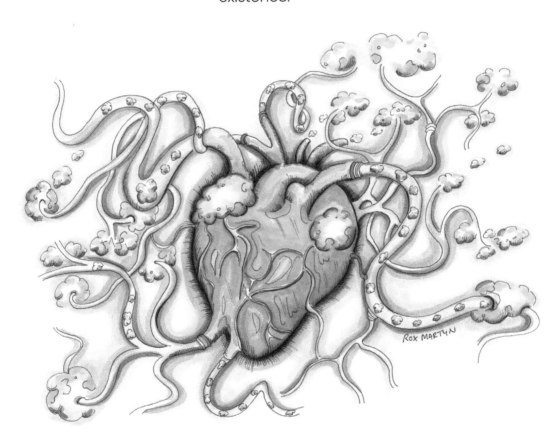

Service Station

Most things,
need regular servicing,
to keep them running smoothly.
Parts get old,
technology evolves,
people, products and processes,
get broken and worn out,
without a doubt,
get cracking!

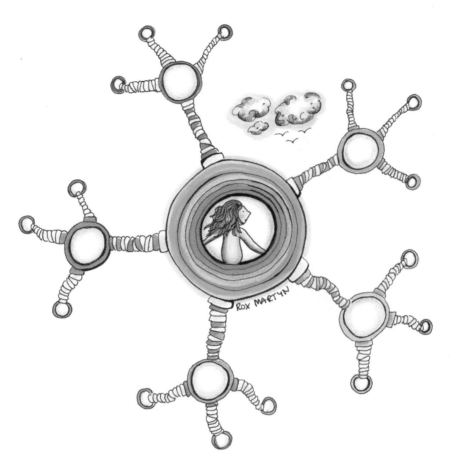

Better Outcomes

More,
better, smarter, bigger,
faster, cheaper, smaller, louder,
making more ridiculous demands,
like obsessive *more*,
maniacs.

What matters more,
for getting a *more valuable* outcome,
is the transformative experience,
that happens to lead,
to the gold.

Success Story

Success,
is somewhat vague,
and may feel unattainable,
without a clear picture,
of our envisioned,
masterpiece.

Tell a story,
of a changed world,
a different and better reality.
Bring people along with you,
from beginning to end,
and beyond.

The Problems We Encounter

Over Control

People,
grow and thrive,
from roots and shoots of trust.
Trying to over control,
our precious golden eggs,
smothers their creative power,
unexplored potential,
and the seeds of bright ideas.
Let the wings of opportunity open,
take flight, explore far and wide,
our expansive world,
of possibility,
beyond.

We Me

We.
Not Me, You or I.
Is how we build connection,
and become a community of creators.
With our respectful, collaborative spirit,
we connect, engage, build and move.
By working better together,
we make good things,
happen.

Step Aside

Sometimes,
it helps to step aside.
We are often our worst enemy,
of change and progress.
The person we see,
stubbornly standing before us,
in the large mirror door,
refusing to budge without reason,
blocks our way, prevents our progress.
A world of opportunity awaits,
if we budge our butts,
and step aside.

Saying No

Knock, knock!
No, thanks.
No.
Simply,
a powerful word,
wonderfully liberating,
if used politely,
and wisely.

No,
protects our integrity,
our values, identity, and sanity,
creating good boundaries for ourselves,
preserving our heart and soul,
for what matters,
more.

Setback Impact

The negative impact,
of seemingly small setbacks,
weigh far heavier than,
the positive impact,
of big wins.

Decisiveness

Decisions,
are the inevitable essence,
of everyday life.
Indecision,
paralyses our progress.
Move swiftly throughout the day,
lighten overwhelming loads.
Organise those decisions wisely,
the time, place and level of priority.
Preserve precious time and energy,
make headspace to think clearly,
and become better, braver,
decision makers.

Stifling Systems

The firm,
creates the system,
the model, the process.
It has the power to create things,
both helpful and unhelpful.
Things,
that grow and stifle, expand and narrow,
unlock and block, open and close.
The way we do things,
shapes the pathways we take,
and places we go.
If we don't like the way,
and become trapped, stifled or stuck,
within the enclosed system,
inhale the scent of possibility,
lurking beyond the exit,
and escape!

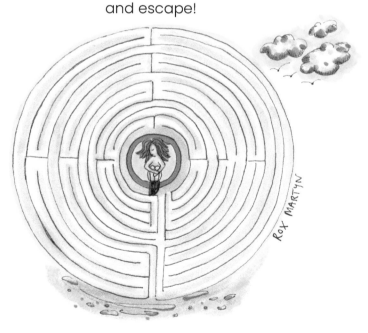

Slow Stagnation

Creativity,
moves us forward.
Stubbornly resisting change,
standing still and silent,
slowly and surely stagnating,
as the waves of change,
wash repeatedly over our heads.
Anchored in one place,
isn't a smart move.
Movement,
is how we stay,
alive.

Communication Breakdown

When,
communication sings,
we orchestrate masterpieces.
When,
communication stalls,
chaos and confusion rises.
And we go,
nowhere.

Lost connection,
leads to communication breakdown,
and loss of power.
Connection,
makes repair possible,
rebooting the powerful engine,
that enables us to travel places,
spark new conversations,
connect and create,
a better way,
forward.

Insufficient Resources

Resource deprived,
our hands may be tied,
as we struggle to construct,
anything meaningful.
Creativity needs,
an infrastructure of resources,
for bright ideas to travel,
and become,
a new way,
of life.

Toxic Cultures

Toxicity,
kills things, and people.
Including creativity and bright ideas,
within people and places.
Blame, shame, bullies,
fear, negativity, criticism, judgement.
The usual parade of ugly offenders,
slowly steal our precious oxygen,
sucking the life and soul,
from creativity.

Dangling Carrots

Bunny Girl,
plonks herself down,
sighs with exhaustion,
and says,
'Please, please, please,
will you please stop,
dangling carrots.
I'm done.'

Buried Heads

Heads buried,
down into the depths of business,
(maybe digging for more carrots)
is no place to notice,
the tension stirring the air above,
distant rumbles of emerging problems,
a new reality unfolding,
on the horizon,
of change.

Our Landscape Of Progress

Orchestrating Creativity

Creativity,
can be tricky to manage.
By understanding, embracing and encouraging,
our extraordinary combined power,
we learn to master,
the art of,
orchestrating creativity,
as a powerful force,
of change.

Thinking Ahead

Life,
business and creativity,
are (a bit) like a game of chess.
We have to think ahead,
to stay in the game.
With eyes fixated on our goal,
we strategically make,
our next move,
forward.

Horticulturalists

Horticulturalists,
know how to grow things.
Human creativity needs,
cultivating,
a thriving ecosystem,
to surface, survive and grow,
engage with the world,
and generously gift us,
with wild and precious fruits,
of wonder.

Maybe,
just maybe,
we should learn to become,
horticulturalists.

Catalysts

Creativity,
is about movement,
keeping us on our toes,
as we travel along,
through life.

Catalysts,
create that movement,
keeping our wheels in motion,
giving power to creativity,
enabling bright ideas,
to rise and flow.

Delivery Vehicles

Bright ideas,
might make us feel,
excited, warm and fuzzy.
But if we fail to make them happen,
to get them on the road,
they will never become anything,
more than a fleeting fuzzy feeling.
Creativity is about action, change and progress,
it needs vehicles to deliver the goods,
to transport bright ideas,
from wild imaginations into the real world,
to begin working their magic,
before we begin,
again.

Making Plans

A big vision,
without a plan to get there,
is merely a lofty dream,
an indulgence for entertaining,
our wild imagination.

A plan,
must be created,
take us places, step by step,
be interesting and challenging,
adoptable, actionable, achievable,
and above all enjoyable.
Enabling a big vision,
to become a new,
reality.

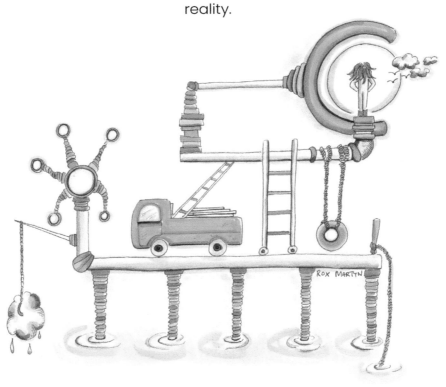

Constant Learning

People,
who stop learning,
become old and obsolete,
out of touch with the world,
and the evolution,
of reality.

Learning,
is how we grow.
Connecting and engaging,
with the world in meaningful ways.
With curiosity, creativity and courage.
Trying and failing, over and over,
upon an infinite rollercoaster,
of constant learning,
we become,
better.

Growing Purposefully

How,
we grow in life,
makes a big difference.
Wild things growing without structure,
become overgrown and chaotic.
With principles to anchor, a purpose to guide,
and values to bind,
we build a lattice to grow gracefully,
encourage meaningful connection,
to shape what we create,
and who we,
become.

Our Community

We belong,
with our people,
culture and community.
People who inspire and challenge us,
to think differently, connect, learn and grow,
become better versions of ourselves.
Sharing stories, curiosities and discoveries,
a little banter over a good coffee.
High five to the similarities,
debate the differences,
of belonging.

Support Network

Useful networks,
provide support and safety,
structure to grow in different ways,
expanding our framework,
our web of possibility,
our climbing frame,
to go places with people,
do brave things,
and begin,
again.

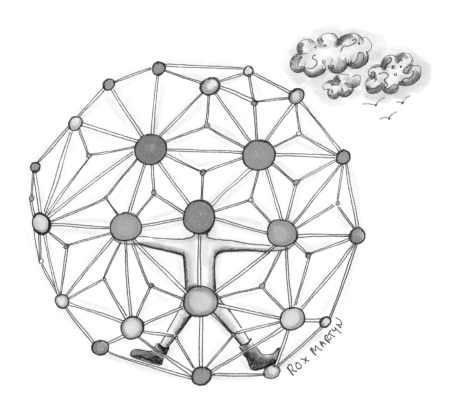

Work In Progress

Creativity,
is work in progress.
There's always something to do,
a problem to solve,
something to repair, improve,
change, invent, reinvent, evolve.
When moving along,
with our rapidly changing world,
creativity will always have,
an important job,
to do.

Small Wins

Seeing progress,
gradually unfurling,
within our contextual landscape,
inspires us to keep going,
endure the marathon.
The motivation of small wins,
key milestones reached, tick,
encouraging signs along the way,
the home stretch looming,
our goal in sight,
getting closer,
and closer,
almost,
there.

Creative Models

Models,
of the business kind,
not the catwalks or kits,
might sound incredibly boring,
but they're the foundations,
upon which progress,
is made.

Creative models,
power us purposefully forward,
with curiosity, creativity and courage,
to explore a bigger picture,
and identify our next opportunity,
to connect with people,
and lead change.
Organisations cannot survive, let alone grow,
without building models,
that embrace,
creativity.

Better Processes

Process, blah!
some people might think,
quickly brushing the thing aside.
But if carefully designed and crafted,
a clever creative process,
transforms,
the way we see, think and feel,
helping to inspire people,
to do better work,
and make better,
things.

Safe Places

Safe places,
enable us to go further.
With solid ground beneath our feet,
we are empowered to take brave steps forward,
travel to the edges of our imagination,
hunting and gathering novel ideas,
and deliver them carefully,
back into reality,
where it's safe,
to land.

Tune Into Relevance

It's easy,
to fade away,
into irrelevance,
if we fail to tune into,
our changing landscape,
new emerging realities,
the natural evolution,
of relevance.

Freedom To Explore

The only way,
to uncover something novel,
is to trust people,
with freedom to explore,
and see where,
they land.

Staying Curious

Staying curious,
gives us a beacon for change.
We might not be able to influence,
the inevitable evolution of human life,
but we can easily entertain,
our wild imagination,
and lifelong,
curiosity.

Natural Adaption

Notice!
Perhaps we can learn,
how creatures naturally adapt,
to their changing environment,
belonging and becoming,
effortlessly evolving,
with the rhythm,
of life.

Collaborative Growth

Together,
with hard work,
calm commitment,
and social courage,
we move in harmony,
to make a valuable impact,
with our contribution.
We harvest and pollinate,
the fruitful ecosystem of life,
gathering the essence of bright ideas,
building our foundations for efficiency,
a natural model of inspiration,
for engineers and scientists.
A place to store and grow,
patiently produce,
liquid gold.

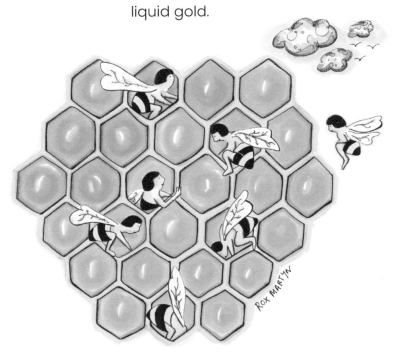

Caring Hands

People,
dance in caring hands,
when they feel safe to move,
creatively expressing thoughts and feelings,
stirring the buried treasures of life,
knowingly supported, encouraged,
respected and valued,
in good hands,
we dance.

Acknowledgements

There are many wonderful, inspiring and influential people in my life. I am grateful to them all for nudging me to think differently, to discover buried creative treasures and bring them into the world. By standing upon their shoulders, they have expanded my landscape of possibility to explore, grow and become a better creator with a gift to share.

This book is a treasure chest of concepts and ideas that have been inspired by first hand experiences and influential creative people. For this, I would like to thank Seth Godin, J.K. Rowling, Brené Brown, Mihaly Csikszentmihalyi, Julia Cameron, Teresa Amabile, Bernadette Jiwa, Elizabeth Gilbert and the late Sir Ken Robinson. This book was seeded by their generous creative brilliance.

Big thanks to my book publisher Ann Wilson at Post Pre-press Group, my editor Samantha Sainsbury and designer Renée Bahr for their encouraging feedback and expertise in making this book happen.

My book assistant, my eight-year-old daughter Billie Grace, has earned many gold stars for inspiring me every day with her curiosity, creativity and courage, for sharing her wonderful ideas and for sprinkling a little colour and creative magic into my world.

I am fortunate to have a lifelong teacher, mentor and friend Liz Lydiate, who has encouraged me to do hard things and been so generous with her time, wisdom and feedback. Liz has nudged me through the grasps of fear and into unknown territory to learn, grow and become a teacher myself.

Heaps of gratitude goes to Sam Margis for teaching me about myself, keeping me on track and preventing me from wandering off the radar, and helping me to navigate the constant flow of challenges in life and business.

Ian Turner, my partner, has endured the consuming process of making this book happen. All the late nights, weekends and holidays of researching, writing and drawing around the clock, and putting up with our home looking like a library/art studio.

Without such kind, caring and generous friends, this book would be forever buried within notes in my ever-growing library of notebooks. For enduring the book marathon by my side, encouraging me to keep going, braving the first draft reviews and giving helpful feedback, I would like to thank Nicola Smith, Megan Sulzberger, Alicia Renfrew and Hillier Deniz. The extended list of friends, beyond the 'book buddies' is too long to mention here but I am hugely grateful to them for bringing their unique rays of sunshine into my life.

I have a rather large family in the UK, where I was born and raised - Mum, my three brothers Scott, Nathan and Leon, three sisters-in-law and nine nieces and nephews. Dad died two years ago and is in my thoughts every day. I draw upon an ever-flowing stream of childhood memories, wonder, adventure, books and plenty of time exploring in nature to feed my creativity and inspire many of the concepts scattered throughout this book.

My Fairy Godmother, Sue Goodwin, and Hannah, have cheered on from afar, sent love and encouraging words when I needed it most. Sam and Marsha Ellias, my 'New York parents', took me under their wing and enabled me to fly into the unknown to experience a different landscape.

There are so many wildly talented people that I have worked with in London, New York, Melbourne and around the world who have inspired and enriched my thinking in so many ways.

And finally, big thanks to all my second homes – the cafés of Elwood and surrounding suburbs in Melbourne, who have watched me frowning and tapping away, reading and drawing, while plying me with the best coffee and food – Miss Alex & Co, Turtle Café, Blue Tongue, Mr Tuppy, Sons Of Mary and Hummingbird.

With gratitudes to you all.

About The Author

Rox Martyn is an emerging voice on business creativity, an artist, facilitator and author. She is a visual thinker and uses her whimsical illustrations to spark conversations, challenge people to think differently and step beyond their comfort zone into a whole world of creative possibility. She has lived and worked in London, New York and Melbourne in equal measures, traversed creative pathways around the world and become a creative business leader. Rox now gathers her life learnings, experiences and insights, and transforms them into 'talking pictures' to inspire people to develop their creative power and potential to move bright ideas into the world. You can engage Rox for creative leadership, speaking events, talks, workshops and creative collaborations.

Photo Credit: Leah Ladson

For more information, please visit:
www.roxmartyn.com
Email: hello@roxmartyn.com
Follow: @roxmartyn

Lightning Source UK Ltd.
Milton Keynes UK
UKHW022355041221
394983UK00002B/203